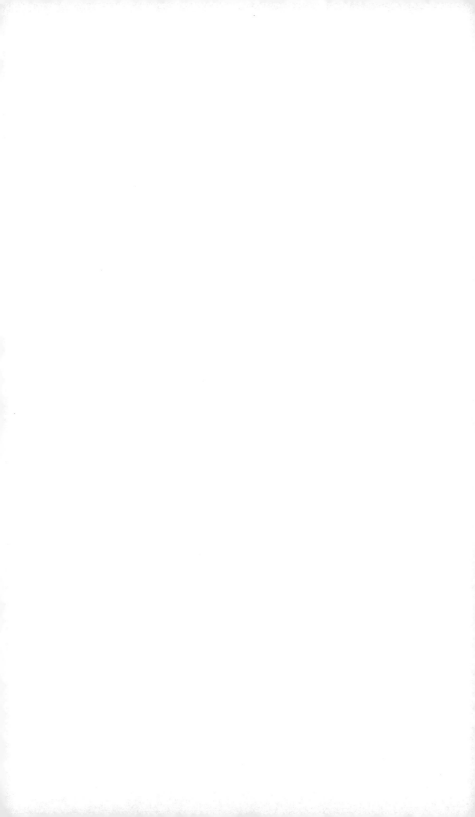

ALDUS
AND HIS
DREAM BOOK

POLIPHILI HYPNEROTOMACHIA, VBI
HVMANA OMNIA NON NISI SO-
MNIVM ESSE OSTENDIT, AT
QVE OBITER PLVRIMA
SCITV SANEQVAM
DIGNA COM-
MEMO.•
RAT.
***
*

ALDUS
AND HIS
DREAM BOOK

An Illustrated Essay

by

Helen Barolini

*

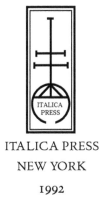

ITALICA PRESS
NEW YORK
1992

ITALICA PRESS, INC.

595 Main Street

New York, New York 10044

Library of Congress Cataloging-in-Publication Data

Barolini, Helen, 1925-
      Aldus and his dream book : an illustrated essay / by Helen Barolini.
         p.   cm.
      Includes bibliographical references and index.
      ISBN 0-934977-22-4 (pbk.).
      1. Manuzio, Aldo, 1449 or 50-1515. 2. Colonna, Francesco, d. 1527. Hypnerotomachia Poliphili. 3. Printing – Italy – Venice – History – Origin and antecedents. 4. Printing – Italy – Venice – History – 16th century.   5. Printers –Italy – Biography. 6. Scholars – Italy – Biography. 7. Editors – Italy – Biography.
      I. Title.
      Z232.M3B19 1991
      070.5'092–dc20
      [B]   91-27624
                                                  CIP

ISBN: 978-0-934977-22-7

Printed in the U.S.A. and E.U.

5 4 3

FOR FURTHER INFORMATION AND
ADDITIONAL TITLES IN RENAISSANCE STUDIES,
VISIT OUR WEBSITE:
WWW.ITALICAPRESS.COM

HYPNEROTOMACHIA POLIPHILI, VBI HV
MANA OMNIA NON NISISOMNIVM
ESSE DOCET . ATQVE OBITER
PLVRIMA SCITV SANE
QVAM DIGNA COM
MEMORAT.

* * *

* *

*

CAVTVM EST, NE QVIS IN DOMINIO
ILL. S. V. IMPVNE HVNC LI
BRVM QVEAT
IMPPRIME
RE .

ABOUT THE AUTHOR

Helen Barolini is the author of the novels *Umbertina* (1979;
1988) and *Love in the Middle Ages* (1986), and *Festa* (1988),
a volume of recipes and recollections of Italian holidays. In
addition to essays and short stories, she has also published translations from the Italian and is the editor of *The Dream Book: An
Anthology of Writings by Italian American Women,* which
received an American Book Award. She has been a Fellow at
the Bellagio Center, Lake Como, Italy.

CONTENTS

NOTE ON THE EDITION

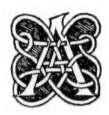 *LDUS AND HIS DREAM BOOK* IS A tribute to the Venetian scholar-publisher of the late fifteenth and early sixteenth centuries, Aldus Manutius. Following up the dramatic innovations of the preceding generation of German printers, Aldus revolutionized the book, leaving us the prototype of the modern printed book, the pocket-sized book, the series of inexpensive classics, italic type and the "old style" of type designs, all of which would survive until today. This project is the outcome of an enthusiasm for Aldus Manutius shared by the publishers and by the author, Helen Barolini, and evolved over the course of many pleasant conversations.

The text of this book is essentially an introduction to Aldus Manutius. Its chapters describe his earliest years, his education, his publishing vision, his book and typo-graphic designs, and his famous Venetian publishing house, the Aldine press. In addition, this book is also an homage to the greatest of all Renaissance illustrated books, the *Hypnerotomachia Poliphili* of Francesco Colonna. This edition attempts to accomplish, with the tools of mod-ern electronic publishing, the same harmony of text, image and proportion that Aldus pioneered. It thus reproduces the

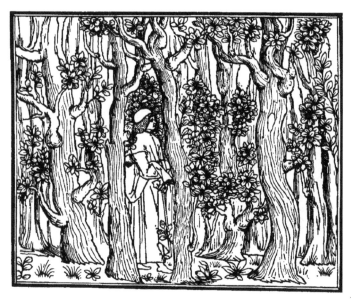

complete illustrations of the first edition of the *Hypnerotomachia Poliphili* in their original order.

* *

*

In preparing this volume copies of the 1499 and 1545 editions from the Aldine press were consulted. These editions differ from one another in several respects, including the placement of woodcuts. The illustrations in the present volume follow the sequence of the woodcuts in the 1499 edition, and they are placed on the pages in relation to the text just as they appeared in the original. In addition, several sequences of the original pages, famous for the harmony and balance between text and graphic, have been reproduced in full. They include THE TRIUMPHS, THE

INSCRIPTIONS, THE GARDENS, THE TROPHIES, and THE
PRECINCT OF VENUS. These pages should appear obvious to
the reader both because of their Italian original and because of
their text's heavier "color." The beauty of these graphics and
their archetypal imagery is such that they harmonize equally well
with both the metal type of the Renaissance and with modern
computer-generated faces.

THE DESIGN OF THIS ESSAY IS ITSELF IN-
TENDED TO REFLECT, BUT NOT SLAVISHLY
IMITATE, THAT OF THE ORIGINAL. THE TYPE-
FACES, MONOTYPE POLIPHILUS AND ADOBE
GARAMOND, WERE CHOSEN FOR THEIR ORI-
GINS IN ALDUS' ORIGINAL TYPEFACE DESIGNS
WITH FRANCESCO GRIFFO, UPON WHICH
GARAMOND AND A HOST

F OLD STYLE FACES ARE BASED.
Although the original edition measures 8″ x
12¼″ – and this work only 5½″ x 8½″ – the
size of the text block in relation to the whole
page, with the resulting white space, is in
proportion to the original. However, the
number of lines per page, thirty-nine in the original edition,
has not been adhered to. In addition to our attempt to retain
the proportion between the page and the accompanying
woodcuts, we have set the text to reflect the original book's
use of blocks of capitals inspired by ancient epigraphy, of
tapering triangles and "vase" shapes to finalize sections
of text, and of decorated initial capitals. We have also

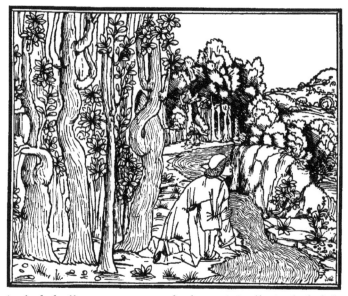

included all two-page spreads that originally included illustrations. In order to preserve the integrity of our text, the
initial capitals are, obviously, not necessarily found on the
same pages in which they originally appeared. As a modern
concession, departing from the Renaissance practice of printing folio numbers on the bottom right of odd pages, running
feet and pagination have been added. When the running foot
includes the symbol: $^*_*$* the page is one of a series of full-page
reproductions that have been chosen for their unity of theme
and beauty of design.

   This book includes notes to the text; a bibliography divided
into sections on Aldus, various editions of the *Hypnerotomachia
Poliphili,* and studies of the *Hypnerotomachia;* a complete list
of illustrations; and an index. The list of illustrations should

prove of great value to students of Colonna's work, both because it provides a key to understanding the iconography of these images; and because, taken together, the captions can give a full narrative of the *Hypnerotomachia* and of its classical themes and interests.

This project is thus not an attempt to reproduce Aldus' *Hypnerotomachia* but to capture the spirit and classic beauty of its design and to introduce to a modern audience of bibliophiles, designers, historians and art historians, and students of myth and archetype this remarkable achievement of Renaissance publishing. We hope, by resetting many of Aldus' page designs, to give the modern reader a sense of the visual and verbal excitement that the Renaissance reader must have felt turning the pages of that milestone in the history of book publishing.

*

THE DESIGN AND LAYOUT of this book were originally facilitated by the generous assistance of the Aldus Corporation. We would again like to thank it and particularly Mr. Brad Stevens of public relations, who responded so enthusiastically to our project, and Paul Brainerd, former President and CEO of Aldus Corporation, whose foreword appears below. Further thanks are offered to Valerie Martone, to Avery Library of Columbia University, and to the New York Public Library's Print Division and Spencer Collection.

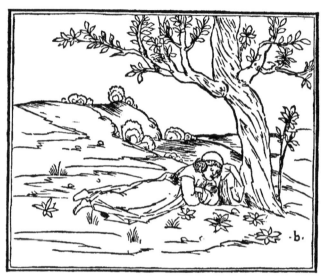

POLIPHILO QVIVI NARRA,CHE GLI PARVE AN-
CORA DI DORMIRE,ET ALTRONDE IN SOMNO
RITROVARSE IN VNA CONVALLE,LAQVALE NEL
FINE ERA SERATA DE VNA MIRABILE CLAVSVRA
CVM VNA PORTENTOSA PYRAMIDE,DE ADMI-
RATIONE DIGNA,ET VNO EXCELSO OBELISCO DE
SOPRA.LAQVALE CVM DILIGENTIA ET PIACERE
SVBTILMENTE LA CONSIDEROE.

LA SPAVENTEVOLE SILVA,ET CONSTI-
pato Nemore euaſo,& gli primi altri lochi per el dolce
ſomno che ſe hauea per le feſſe & proſternate mébre diſ-
fuſo relicti,me ritrouai di riouo in uno piu delectabile
ſito aſſai piu che el præcedente.Elquale non era de mon
ti horridi,& crepidinoſe rupe intorniato, ne falcato di
ſtrumoſi iugi. Ma compoſitamente de grate montagniole di non tropo altecia. Siluoſe di giouani quercioli, di roburi,fraxini & Carpi-
ni,& di frondoſi Eſculi,& Ilice,& di teneri Coryli,& di Alni,& di Ti
lie,& di Opio,& de infructuoſi Oleaſtri,diſpoſiti ſecondo laſpecto de
gli arboriferi Colli. Et giu al piano erano grate ſiluule di altri ſiluatici

arboſcelli,& di floride Geniſte,& di multiplice herbe uerdiſſime, quiui
uidi il Cythiſo, La Carice, la commune Cerinthe. La muſcariata Pana-
chia el fiorito ranunculo,& ceruicello, o uero Elaphio, & la ſeratula,& di
uarie aſſai nobile,& de molti altri proficui ſimplici,& ignote herbe & fio
ri per gli prati diſpenſate. Tutta queſta læta regione de uiridura copioſa-
mente adornata ſe offeriua. Poſcia poco piu ultra del mediano ſuo, io ritrouai uno ſabuleto, o uero glareoſa plagia, ma in alcuno loco diſperſa-
mente, cum alcuni ceſpugli de herbatura. Quiui al gliochii mei uno io-
cundiſſimo Palmeto ſe appræſento, cum le foglie di cultrato mucrone
ad tanta utilitate ad gli ægyptii, del ſuo dolciſſimo fructo fœcūde & abun
dante. Tra lequale racemoſe palme,& picole alcune, & molte mediocre,
& laltre drite erano & excelſe, Electo Signo de uictoria per el reſiſtere ſuo
ad lurgente pondo. Ancora & in queſto loco non trouai incola, ne altro
animale alcuno. Ma peregrinando ſolitario tra le non denſate, ma inter-
uallate palme ſpectatiſſime, cogitando delle Rachelaide, Phaſelide, & Li
byade, non eſſere forſa a queſte comparabile. Ecco che uno affermato &
carniuoro lupo alla parte dextra, cum la bucca piena mi apparue.

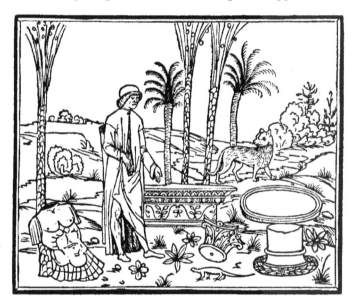

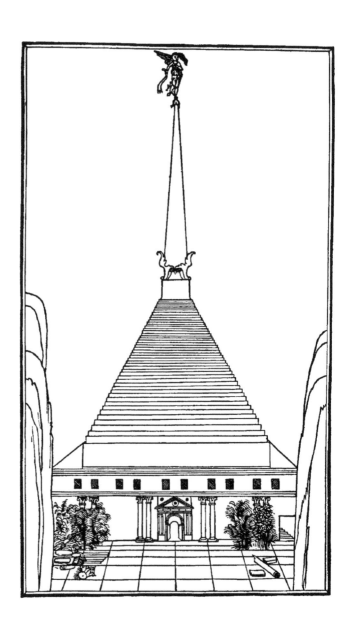

* *
 *   HELEN BAROLINI XVI

FOREWORD

PRINTING TECHNIQUES AND PRACTICES HAVE advanced so dramatically in the past forty-five years that we often forget that they remained virtually unchanged for five hundred years between Gutenberg's introduction of movable type and the advent of electronic prepress technology in the 1960s. Even with recent technological advancements, the innovations of these fifteenth-century pioneers still serve as yardsticks by which we measure today's printing standards. It is a testament to their vision and commitment to improving the way people communicated.

One of these Renaissance printing pioneers, Aldus Manutius, has become an inspiration for modern printing technology. Aldus based his new approaches to publishing on recent technological developments of his time, namely the Gutenberg press. He introduced innovations such as the small book format, italicized type, and standardized punctuation to make books more accessible to the average person. He was committed to establishing a new form of communication that would empower people. He was also committed to excellence, which manifested itself in the endless hours he spent experimenting with typefaces and in the fine quality of his books. Most importantly, he had the courage to introduce his innovations into a publishing world that was averse to change.

When I joined forces with four software engineers in 1984, our goal, like Aldus' five hundred years earlier, was to redefine the way people communicated. We had a vision of producing an inexpensive microcomputer software tool that would allow people to easily combine text and graphics on a page – in short, desktop publishing.

We faced many challenges in the early days, not the least of which was finding a name for our company. We were introducing a new form of publishing and in the process creating a new market. Our name needed to reflect that. We considered a hundred or more names, but nothing worked for us.

We took a trip to Washington and Oregon to test the feasibility of our software with newspaper publishers. Still searching for a name, we spent some free time during this trip in the Oregon State University library in Corvallis. The reference librarian helped us locate books on the history of printing and publishing. That afternoon, we "met" Aldus Manutius for the first time and something clicked.

The parallels were immediately evident. Like Aldus, we were basing our new approach to publishing on the recent technological

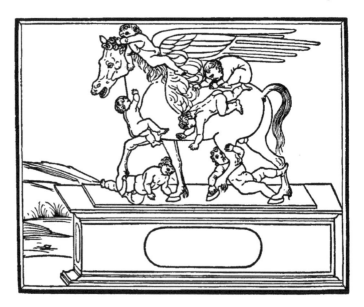

advancements of our time. For us these were the microcomputer and the laser printer rather than the Gutenberg press.

Like Aldus, we added innovations, such as an electronic pasteboard and a floating toolbox that combined with other capa-bilities to make publishing more accessible to the average person. Aldus' concern for quality and innovation were the same values that we felt were important for our new organization.

After reading an early draft of Helen Barolini's manuscript for *Aldus and His Dream Book,* I was once again struck by these parallels, which are even more intriguing given that this book is produced with PageMaker, the software for which Aldus served as an inspiration. It is a fascinating twist, and a fitting tribute, that Aldus' life is reintroduced to a twentieth-century audience with the help of the kind of breakthrough technology he might have developed had he had access to microcomputers half a millennium ago.

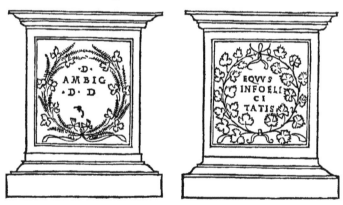

Paul Brainerd
President, Aldus Corporation
Seattle, WA, 1991

PREFACE

DURING THOSE FORTUNATE AND HAPPY
years when I lived in Italy, I was able to pursue an interest in

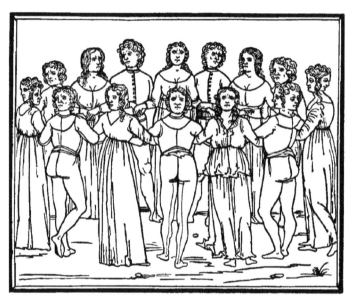

Aldus Manutius, which had begun some years earlier at Columbia University when, to relieve the tedium of required Library
School courses, I took an elective course on Incunabula and
Rare Books. My special area became the Aldine press with its
background of fifteenth-century printing.

*

IT WAS ONLY NATURAL that when my husband's
work took us to his country, Italy, I continued my Aldus

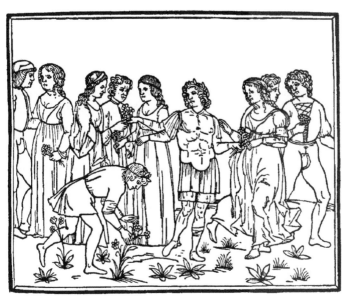

avocation. We lived in Rome, and I was able to attend the
Scuola Vaticana di Paleografia held in the quarters known as
the Archivio Segreto Vaticano. The paleography course covered
the ancient and medieval forms of writing in documents and
inscriptions and was attended by what seemed mostly scholarly
priests and nuns, who would continue in the Scuola for two years
and take exams to qualify them for diplomas as Paleograph-Ar-
chivists. That was not my intention fortunately; the few months
that I followed the course gave me a summary notion of the hands
used in manuscripts, how the great codices were put together,
how to read inscriptions, abbreviations, joined letters, and how
to tell by internal clues the provenance of manuscripts from such
and such a scriptorium at whatever monastery, or when letters
lost their purity of form and fell into decadence.

It was demanding, mysterious, esoteric study far beyond my ability to master, and it confirmed me in my admiration for those who pursue and master such knowledge and for Aldus who, in pursuit of his goal to print all the extant classics of Greece, various ancient Latin classics, and medieval texts, had to peruse often barely decipherable parchments and to unravel the hurried and abbreviated hands they were written in, or to bring to light the text of palimpsests. I remember the jolt I felt at learning that *misericordia* could show up in manuscripts as $\overline{mia}$, or even $\overline{ma}$. It would take a lifetime to learn to decipher all the shortcuts the scribes took! I still have my notes from the Scuola; they still awe me. What supreme patience, what art and skill to unravel all those old documents of the past through which our civilization and culture were preserved and transmitted. What we take for granted, in our plethora of the printed word, is the end result of centuries of preservation and transmission.

My husband and I and our family spent one memorable summer on the Lido across from Venice where he worked on his novel, our children went to the beach, and I explored the sites of Aldus' press and home and used the resources of the Marciana Library. From Rome to Venice, I saw to it that we made Aldus stops along the way. We went to Carpi where Aldus had been in the employ of the princely family, and there, in the castle, now a Civic Museum, was Aldus depicted in a chapel mural. We saw Ferrara where Aldus studied and later found refuge. Back in Rome, I made my way both to Aldus' birthplace in nearby Bassiano and to the birthplace of book printing in Italy at the Benedictine monastery of Santa Scholastica at Subiaco.

To be able to remember Aldus again in this work has been another excursion of pleasure.

Helen Barolini

I. PRINTING COMES TO ITALY

IN A PRINT THAT ACCOMPANIES PROSPER
Marchand's *Histoire de l'origine et des premiers progrès de
l'imprimerie* of 1740, the spirit of printing is shown descending from the heavens under the aegis of Minerva and Mercury.
Printing is given first to Germany, who then presents it to female
figures representing Holland, England, Italy and France, each of
whom holds a medallion portrait of her country's master printers. Germany displays Gutenberg and Fust, the first to employ

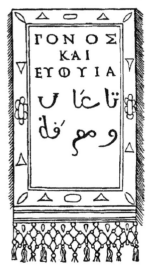

movable type in the printing of
books; Italy, the likeness of Aldus
Manutius, who was to expand the
initial invention into the prototype of
the modern book and in the process
set international standards for the
newborn art of book printing and
publishing.

Aldo Manuzio was probably
born in 1449/50. As with kings,
popes, saints, and great artists, his fame
made him known to the world simply
by his first name, latinized into Aldus,
in accord with the humanist fashion of
his time. At its full extent, his name was
styled Aldus Pius Manutius Romanus, the Pius being an honorific
bestowed on him by Prince Alberto Pio of Carpi to whom Aldus
had been tutor, and the Romanus for his association with Rome where
he had studied as a young man, and one imagines, for the classical
overtones it conferred.

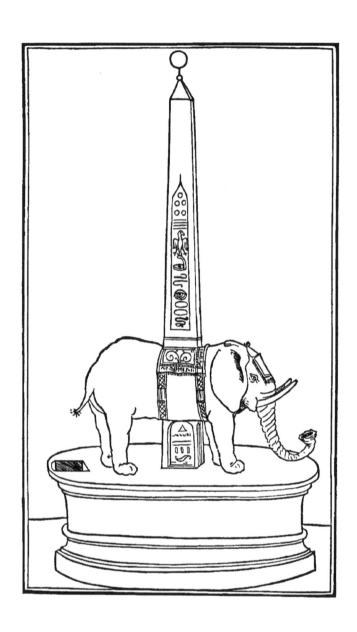

Aldus, a humanist scholar as well as a printer-publisher, recovered and printed the classics in authoritative texts; he introduced italic type, set up editorial standards, aided the dissemination of humanist learning in the West, launched the modern book, and gave the world that period's most beautiful expression of printed book art when he combined text with woodcut illustrations in the exquisite and intriguingly arcane romance, Francesco Colonna's *Hypnerotomachia Poliphili.*

Aldus' dates (1449/50-1515), his presence in Venice at a period when the Serene Republic was the meeting place of Eastern and

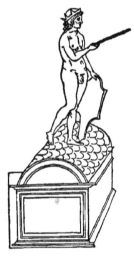

אם לא כי הבהמה   כסתה את בשרי
אזי הייתי ערום חפש ותמצא הגיוני

ΓΥΜΝΟΣ ΗΝ ,ΕΙ ΜΗ ΑΝ ΘΗΡΙ-
ΟΝ ΕΜΕΚΑΛΥΥΕΝ.ΖΗΤΕΙ.ΕΥ-
ΡΗΣΗΔΕ.ΕΑΣΟΝ ΜΕ.

NVDVS ESSEM, BESTIANIME
TEXISSET.QVAERE.ET INVE
NIES.MESINITO.

Western culture, his work as publisher, and his interchange with many of the notable figures of the period make him a nexus for many aspects of Renaissance history. Aldus lived at the height of humanism, when scholars and popes were expanding Petrarch's passion for classical literature, and when the arts of humane learning and living flourished under the patronage of the famous princely courts of Italy.

The clients of the Aldine press included Federigo Gonzaga, Isabella d'Este, Lucrezia Borgia, and the Medici pope, Leo X; among Aldus' pupils were the future poet Ercole Strozzi and diplomat Prince Alberto Pio of Carpi; friends included the lights of Renaissance learning – Giovanni Pico della Mirandola

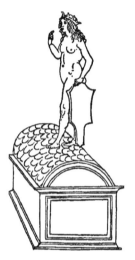

היה מי שתהיה   קח מן האוצר וזה כאות ונפש!

אבל אזהיר אותך הסר הראש ואל תיגע בגופו

OΣTIΣ EI . ΛABE EK TOYΔE
TOYΘHΣAYPOY,OΣON AN A
PEΣKOI.ΠAPAINΩΔEΩΣ ΛA-
BHıΣ THN KEΦAΛHN . MH A
ΠTOY ΣΩMATOΣ.

QVISQVIS ES, QVANTVN
CVNQVE LIBVERIT HV-
IVS THESAVRI SVME AT-
MONEO . AVFER CAPVT.
CORPVS NE TANGITO.

and Erasmus of Rotterdam, the poets Bembo and Poliziano, the bibliophile Jean Grolier, the Venetian nobleman and chronicler Marin Sanudo. Aldus corresponded with William Latimer, the English humanist who was pursuing studies at the University of Padua, and speaks with esteem in a preface of the redoubt-able Thomas Linacre as the brilliant exception to what Aldus referred to as the general uncouthness of England at the time.

* *

*

IT WAS IN A WEALTHY, trade-oriented, liberally governed, cosmopolitan Venice[1] that Aldus first set up his press, for not only the roads of commerce and enterprise led to Venice, but also the burgeoning book trade and the influx of Hellenistic scholars. Printing had started in Venice in 1469 when John of Speyer, a German, opened his press. From 1469 until Aldus' death in 1515 spans almost half a century; it starts just after and reaches just beyond that period of the printed book's infancy when the first exemplars were fittingly identified as *incunabula*, the Latin plural of "cradle," to designate the book's infancy. From the publication of Gutenberg's

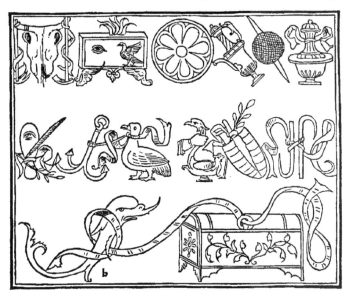

Bible in 1455 to the end of the fifteenth century is what print historians call the true *incunabula* period, and it was in 1499 that the *Hypnerotomachia Poliphili* issued from the Aldine press. As George Painter, Assistant Keeper in charge of Incunabula at the

British Museum, wrote, "Gutenberg's 42-line Bible of 1455 and the *Hypnerotomachia Poliphili* of 1499 confront one another from opposite ends of the incunable period with equal and contrasting pre-eminence. The Gutenberg Bible is sombrely and sternly German, Gothic, Christian and medieval; the *Hypnerotomachia* is radiantly and graciously Italian, classic, pagan and renascent. These are the two supreme masterpieces of the art of printing, and stand at the two poles of human endeavour and desire."[2]

The last half of the fifteenth century was a time of typographical innovations, of a wide range of reading matter made available, of investigation into sources, of the ascendancy of text over the authority of the master-teacher. It helped produce the century of genius; it was the beginning of what Marshall McLuhan will term the linear-print culture.[3] Elizabeth Eisenstein in *The Printing Revolution in Early Modern Europe* makes the connection between the divulgation possible through the printing press and the advance of science: "As a contemporary of Aldus Manutius, Copernicus had an opportunity to survey a wider range of records and to use more reference guides than had any astronomer before him.... Given freedom from many hours of 'slavish' copying, given an increased output of dictionaries and other reference guides, given title pages, book lists, and other rudimentary bibliographical aids, Copernicus was able to undertake a search of the literature on a vaster scale than had been possible before...he was supplied...with guidance to technical literature carefully culled from the best Renaissance Greek manuscript collections and, for the first time, made available outside library walls."[4]

*

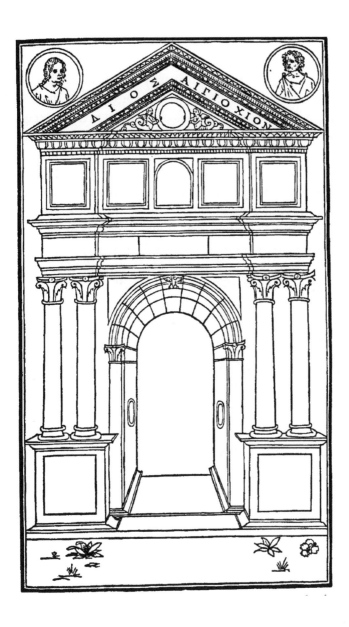

ALTHOUGH IT WAS TO VENICE that the Frenchman Jenson and Germans like Ratdolt came to set up their presses, it is interesting to note that a monastery in the Sabine hills outside Rome was the site of the first book printed in Italy. Rome was first in the illustration of books, and Milan in the printing of Greek letter. Yet each expansion of the printing art was taken up at Venice and received its highest development there. Not only was Venice supreme in the number of fifteenth-century printers practicing there,[5] but also, for a time in her history, for the richness and beauty of the volumes her printers produced. As an Italian source notes concerning Venice, "book art reaches

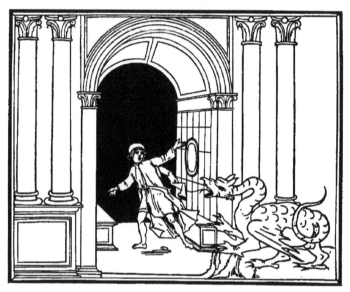

here the height of perfection, as much for the elegance and variety of type, for the exquisiteness of ornamental borders and woodcut illustrations, for the quality of paper, as for textual care and correctness."[6]

Johann Gutenberg's great achievement seems, like all great inventions, obvious once it has been accomplished. The general principles of movable type were already known in Gutenberg's day — and illustrated "books" were printed from wooden blocks for the populace of Northern Europe — but no purposeful and practical adaptation had been forthcoming until Gutenberg's long and patient tinkering with cast type found its application in the printed book. Gutenberg's process was to set type into frames to produce identical, multiple impressions — the enormous step in intellectual history of establishing standard texts over the frequently disparate and corrupted manuscripts, which were hand-copied by scribes liable to all the errors of fatigue, distraction, willful emendation and, yes, ignorance.

What printers initially produced, however, were folio volumes that were still as large, expensive, unwieldy, and inaccessible to a large public as were the manuscripts that preceded printing and continued to co-exist alongside the printed book for almost another century. Through the incunabula period, and well after the close of the fifteenth century, the printed volume was on the defensive against the magnificent, bejeweled, gold-leafed, hand-written books on vellum and parchment, which were the exclusive prerogatives of wealthy patrons or monastery collections. The first printed books were greeted with a mix of surprise for the novelty, but also disdain for its unpleasant origins — born out of a lowly press by way of bad-smelling ink and paper made from rags and glue. The printed book seemed a crude thing in comparison to the glories of the illuminated manuscripts. Federigo da Montefeltre (1422-82), the first duke of Urbino, whose palace was to become the model of the idealized Renaissance court in Castiglione's *The Courtier,* declared he "would have been ashamed to own a printed book."[7] By the time his son Guidobaldo (1472-1508) was the reigning duke, it was a different story. Guidobaldo was a collector of books from the Aldine press, and the most impressive issue from that press, indeed of all fifteenth-century printing – Francesco Colonna's *Hypnerotomachia Poliphili* – was dedicated to him.

T FIRST PRINTERS TRIED TO EMU-late the great folio volumes in order to insure the patronage of the wealthy; they printed on large sheets leaving large white margins and often empty spaces on the pages where initial letters of a para-graph could be put in hand by rubricators to offer some color and eye-appeal. These incunabula were stately tomes, and even today the crisp white sheets of the fine hand-laid paper are marvelous to behold. But such books were as beyond reach of most readers as the manuscripts they replaced. Aldus, too, produced such large and expensive books for collectors until, in 1501, with the introduction of Virgil's *Georgics* in octavo format, he produced the modern book – lower in price, convenient in size.

* *
*

THE FIRST PRINTERS in Italy were Conrad Sweinheim and Arnold Pannartz, two workers from Mainz in the employ of Johann Fust and Peter Schoeffer – the partners who took over the bankrupt Gutenberg press. Sweinheim and Pannartz journeyed the Benedictines' old trans-Alpine route linking Mainz with Italy until they got to Subiaco in the mountain fasts of the

Aniene River valley some forty-seven miles east of Rome. There they set up their printing press in the monastery of Santa Scholastica where St. Benedict had founded his order. They had borne on their journey the literal weight of the tools of their trade. Strong traditional ties existed between Mainz and Subiaco, for German monks were a presence in the Italian monastery since at least a century earlier.[8] When Sweinheim and Pannartz arrived at the abbey in 1464, ten out of its eighteen monks were German, including the prior, thus relieving them of any language problems in a foreign land.

It is thought that the pair might have been invited to Subiaco by Spanish cardinal Juan de Torquemada – whose nephew Tomás de Torquemada was to become the infamous Inquisitor General of Spain under whom the Jews were expelled in 1492 – a strong defender of papal power who in 1456 had been given the administration of the abbey at Subiaco by his countryman,

PATIENTIA EST ORNAMENTVM CVSTODIA
ET PROTECTIO VITAE.

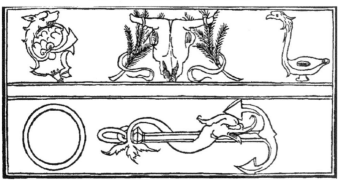

the first Borgia pope, Calixtus III. The cardinal was renowned for his theological learning and might well have seen the infant press as an instrument for the propagation of doctrine. Sweinheim and Pannartz, on the other hand, would have found Subiaco, in the pontifical states, inviting as a place of peace and relative tranquility after the sack of Mainz in 1462 hastened the spread of printing from its original center. Even before the turmoil of the city's sack, Mainz was not the place to put into print anything "unsafe." Lehmann-Haupt makes this clear in noting the decided paucity of humanist texts and the total absence of scientific works on Schoeffer's list of publications, or on the list of any other Mainz printer.

Sweinheim and Pannartz remained in Subiaco until 1467 and while there printed four volumes, the first printed in Italy, or, for that, matter, anywhere outside of Germany.[9] They were followed in Italy by other German printers eager to make a business of the new printing invention in the thriving cities of
Italy. Venice has always been a natural point of arrival
for Germans coming over the Alps to Italy; so many
of the itinerant printers settled in Venice and set
up shop there that soon a whole quarter
of the city, Fondaco dei
Tedeschi, was
named for
them.
*

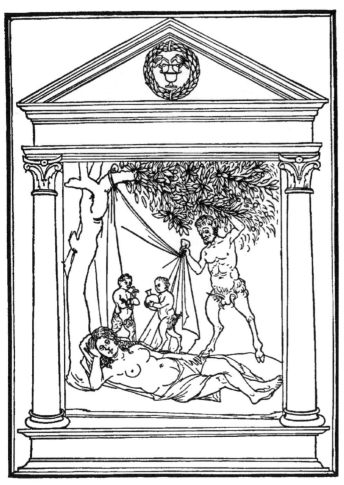

ΠΑΝΤΩΝ ΤΟΚΑΔΙ

IN 1469, a document in Venetian state archives shows that Venice granted John of Speyer, a Bavarian, an exclusive privilege to print in that city. John of Speyer was not a novice of printing,

but a master of the new art. The colophon of his first publication, a folio volume of Cicero's *Epistolae familiares,* proudly
declares the priority of his press in Venice. It is interesting to

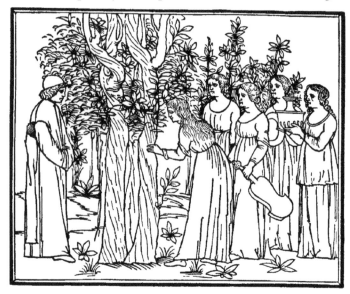

note that in this volume, passages that required Greek letter
are left blank, to be filled in by hand by the purchaser, or by a
copyist for him.

The results of Venice's granting a fiveyear monopoly on
printing to John of Speyer would have surely impeded the book
trade in that city if the printer's untimely death in 1470, after just
a year of activity, had not annulled the grant. Thenceforth printers
flocked to this Adriatic city that offered more freedom – especially
from ecclesiastic authority – than any other in Italy.

Aldus Manutius' road to Venice was to be a long one; his
first road led from Bassiano to Rome.

II. ALDUS' EARLIEST YEARS

ALDUS' BIRTHPLACE, THE VILLAGE OF Bassiano in the Alban hills, about thirty-five miles southeast of Rome, was part of the duchy of Sermoneta held by the Roman princely family of Caetani. The village numbers less than two thousand inhabitants, and even today Bassiano figures in no gazetteer, Baedeker, atlas, or tourist account. It was, nonetheless, recalled by Aldus himself in some early Greek editions when he attached "Basianas" to his name, and in his own personal correspondence when he referred to himself as *civis bassianatis,* a citizen of Bassiano.

The year of Aldus' birth is debated. Some estimates have varied from 1445 to 1449 based on Erasmus' erroneous calculations. Most scholars now agree on 1449 or 1450. The evidence comes from a reference made by Aldus' grandson, Aldus the Younger, in a preface to a work that he published in Rome in 1597, wherein he makes reference to it being 147 years since his predecessor's birth.[11]

Though much about Aldus is open to speculation, some things can be gleaned from his chatty prefaces, his correspondence, and documents such as his wills and petitions. Aldus remembered his birthplace in his wills, the last of which, dated 1515 the year he died, left twelve nubile girls of Bassiano (of whom six were to be his nieces or other relatives) twenty-five ducats each as a dowry.

Bassiano itself did not remember Aldus until 1965, on the commemoration of the 450th year since his death. Then his birthplace decided to erect a monument to its most famous native son. The memorial bust with its suitable inscription quoting Aldus' own words – "for the abundance of good books which, we hope, will finally put to flight all ignorance" – honors his printing achievements and humanist goals. It is placed in front of the ancient stone wall around the grey town, which seems not to have changed its aspect in the five centuries since his birth there. Aldus' bust looks away from the grim town and towards the wooded mountains beyond which lies Subiaco where, in Aldus' youth, Sweinheim and Pannartz were setting up the first press in Italy. Or perhaps Aldus' gaze is towards Rome – a far-reaching look that he may often have indulged in as a boy dreaming of the Eternal City and what knowledge could be gained there.

In the town, affixed to a modest dwelling on Via Aldo Manuzio, is a plaque placed on behalf of the people of Bassiano and dated July 3, 1966, stating that tradition has it that Aldo Manuzio, greatest of the humanist editors, was born in that house *("in questa casa a metà del secolo XV è tradizione nascesse Aldo Manuzio sommo editore umanista").* It is a cautious rendition cast in a subjunctive that skirts certainty. Not anyone can now attest absolutely that this building was home to Aldus, so it is laid to tradition. The fact that he was a most excellent humanist and publisher is beyond doubt and stated forthrightly.

* *

*

NOTHING is known of the young Aldo Manuzio and his life in Bassiano except for a passing reference in the preface to his *Rudimenta grammatices latinae linguae,* where Aldus mentions his very earliest training in Latin as coming from a local teacher inept in the art of grammar who had him memorize verses from the *Doctrinale,* a very popular school book in the fifteenth century, which went through 279 editions until the last one appeared in 1588.[12]

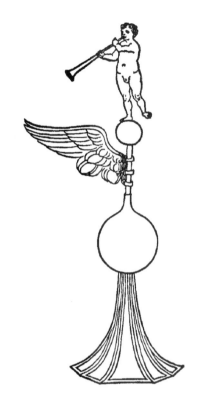

From oblique evidence in the documents of the Caetani family archives, it seems that one of Aldus' ancestors was a bishop of Venafro who, however, managed to father three sons to whom he left inheritances, and one of whom became involved with his Caetani overlord, resulting in a confiscation of holdings that were then restored under a later Caetani.[13] These shadowy allusions serve only to support the speculation that Aldus came from a family of some means and some education. Possibly with some recommendations from the Caetani family, or from clerics in the area, Aldus left Bassiano to get on in the world.

III. ALDUS IN ROME

IN THE SECOND HALF OF THE FIFTEENTH century the world was in papal Rome, and there Aldus went to study. Though Aldus in Rome remains a vague figure, the city itself was a magnificent presence. Those who lived that Renaissance period of Rome's glory – approximately covering the period from the Holy Year of 1450 to the sack of Rome in 1527 – were aware of a rebirth of learning and saw enough change to be cognizant of the contrast between their age and the preceding one.

It was a time when Italy was in full flower of the humanist revival of classical learning[14]: Cosimo de' Medici, first of that family to rule Florence, was midway in a reign so auspicious for that city that at his death Florence would commemorate him with the title *Pater Patriae,* anticipating by several centuries George Washington's own title as Father of his Country; in Milan in 1450 Francesco Sforza was invested with the ducal title, thus initiating that family's rule; the Venetian Republic was rich and powerful and enjoying an enlightened pragmatism that encouraged all aspects of trade; and in Rome Pope Nicholas V, who as the modest monk Tommaso Parentucelli had incurred debt by buying or having copied manuscripts of the classics, fulfilled his humanist inclination, when raised to the papacy in 1447, by establishing his reputation as a scholar, a patron of learning, the rebuilder of Rome, and the founder of the Vatican Library.

There was a climate of ferment, intellectual bedazzlement – and the tensions of uncertainty. Times were changing. With Dante, medieval thought and structure had reached culmination in its greatest monument, *The Divine Comedy.* And with

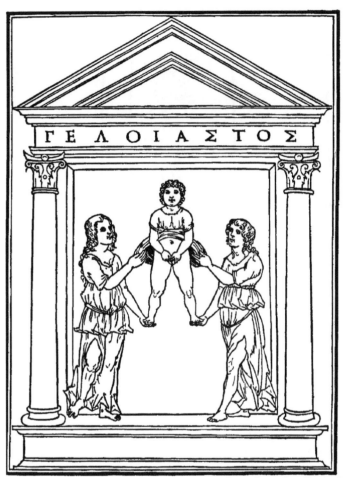

Dante, too, comes the first indication of modern intellectual temperament and feelings beautifully expressed in the Ulysses episode of the *Inferno* (Canto 26). It is the poet's very human understanding of Ulysses the man and his ardor *a divinir del*

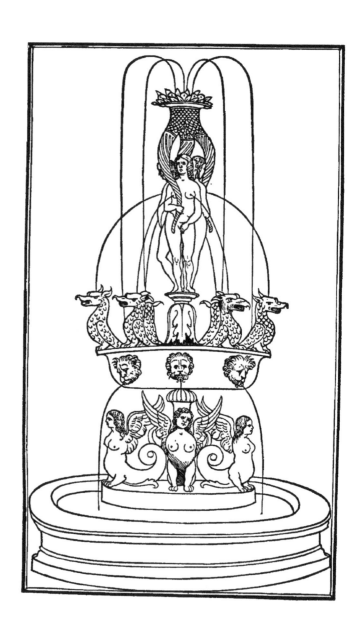

mondo esperto, / e delle vizi umani e del valore (to taste all experience and to know the ways and worth of humankind), that places Dante on the threshold of the modern era. Humanism lay ahead, the great opening to learning and recovery of knowledge that was fulfilled and fixed with the advent of printing and the dissemination of books. Dante, the medieval-classicist, with his serene contemplation of the Greek and Roman eras and his placing himself in the company of the great classical poets, prepared the way. *The Divine Comedy* anticipates the reflowering of classical learning, as embodied in Virgil, the guide, as much as it is the final paean to scholasticism.

It is Francesco Petrarca (Petrarch, 1304-74) who is known as the first humanist, for it was his searching out of lost classical manuscripts and his passion for what they contained that set the climate for the growing revival of classical learning in Italy. Petrarch revived the literary classical style and spirit of Latin literature. He also attempted to learn Greek from the monk Barlaam, a bishop in Calabria, which had been a part of the ancient Magna Graecia where Greek was still spoken.

Historically, a goal of the humanists, led by Petrarch, to search out lost and forgotten classical manuscripts and to acquire enough skill to read the Greek ones, was abetted by the influx of Greek scholars into Italy during the Council of Florence-Ferrara, which in 1438-45 attempted reconciliation between the Greek and Roman churches. An apex was reached during Nicholas V's reign, when Constantinople fell to the Turks in 1453, resulting in an exodus of Greeks to Italy and with them their language and literature. Before the end of Nicholas' reign, printing – that new "adventure and art" as

Gutenberg called it[15] — was given to a Western world ready to use it to disseminate the recovered Latin and Greek classics.

* *

*

THERE IS A PASSAGE in the *Cologne Chronicle*, published in 1499, that refers to printing as having been investigated until 1450, "a Golden Year when men began to print, and the first book that was printed was the Bible in Latin." The chronicler, in his enthusiasm for the new invention, wanted the significance of 1450, being a Holy Year, to shed its luster also on printing. The "Golden Year" means the Holy Year, so-called from the papal decree initiating it in 1300 and designating the beginning of a new century as a commemorative time for celebrating in Rome a jubilee that granted special indulgences to pilgrims traveling there.[16] It was then advanced to the mid-century in 1450 by Nicholas V to mark the end of papal schism after the submission of the Council of Basel, and its anti-pope, to the authority of Rome in 1449. If 1450 is taken as the year of Aldus' birth, the luster of that jubilee year can be extended to him, too.

Enormous throngs traveled to Rome, and among the attractions was the canonization of the popular preacher, San Bernardino of Siena. Great hordes of arriving pilgrims converged on the bridge of Sant'Angelo, crossing the Tiber to St. Peter's and recalling Dante's vivid description of such a jubilee mob as part of hell—*Inferno* XVIII: 28-32. The pilgrims' offerings swelled Nicholas' coffers and gave visible proof of the pope's restored authority in Rome.

Nicholas V, a former librarian of Cosimo de' Medici and a scholar of great learning, reigned from 1447 to 1455. Another

Renaissance intellect, Aeneas Sylvius Piccolomini, who later became Pope Pius II, said of Nicholas V, "What he does not know is outside the range of human knowledge." He became a patron of the arts and vigorously cultivated learning by commissioning new editions of Latin classics and translations from the Greek. A fortune was spent in searching out and buying the almost one thousand antique codices of Nicholas' personal

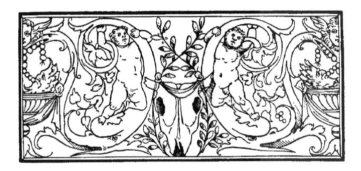

collection, which was to become the nucleus of the Vatican Library. He made Rome the center of humanism, attracting those like Aldo Manuzio who went there for his beginning studies. The pope's own circle included the foremost intellects of the time – such arresting men as Leon Battista Alberti, Gian Francesco Poggio Bracciolini, and Lorenzo Valla. Alberti, a many talented, quintessential Renaissance man, prototype, indeed, of the species, was so skilled a Latinist that a comedy he wrote as a young man was "rediscovered" and published in 1588 by Aldus the Younger as the lost classical work of Lepidus Comicus.

Concurrent with Nicholas V's reign, Johann Gutenberg, after long years of experimentation with punches, type, ink, press and paper, printed first his Donatus grammar in 1448 and then the splendid 42-line Bible at Mainz in 1455. The humanist pope himself was to be represented in print: letters of indulgence bearing dates and now considered to be some of the earliest work ascribed to Gutenberg were printed in 1454-55. The earliest printed and dated document in Europe is the three-line Indulgence of 1454 granted by Nicholas V to those who donated money for the struggle against the Turks.

*

RENOUARD,[17] the redoubtable French scholar of Aldus, notes that when Aldus left his country teacher, he went on to study Latin in Rome with Gaspare da Verona. Most prob-

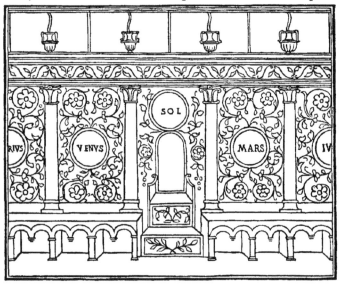

ably he boarded in the home of his teacher, as was the custom in those days. He would have paid for his room, board, and instruction and shared the life of his master – a simple one enlivened, perhaps, by the accounts of current feuds among the humanists and papal retribution. It was as a private teacher to a group of pupils like Aldus that Gaspare da Verona made his living. Professors of eloquence (under which rubric was gathered the subject-matter of humanism) were rarely fixtures at universities, as were the professors of law, medicine and theology. "Their position," says Symonds, "was always that of wandering stars and resident aliens."[18] And yet they were indispensable in that society as secretaries, house tutors, readers, historiographers, public orators, editors for the new printing houses, and private teachers.

There are no documented dates for this period in young Aldus' life, but it can be deduced that he was in Rome from about 1465 to at least 1473, the year Gaspare da Verona retired from teaching. Domizio Calderini, also of Verona, a city that Aldus hails as "the mother and muse of erudite men," was only four years older than Aldus. It is recorded that he died of the plague at age thirty-two in 1478.[19] He is said to have been a man of prodigious activity and unbounded knowledge who was called to Rome by Pope Paul II to be public professor at the University of Rome. Aldus does not refer to Calderini as his private teacher, nor are any dedications of Aldine editions made to him, as with Gaspare da Verona and Aldus' later teacher in Ferrara, Battista Guarino; but from a statement in his preface to his 1502 edition of Statius, in which he speaks of hearing Domizio Calderini, it can be surmised that Aldus probably attended Calderini's public lectures. What we do know, from Aldus' own testimony, is the warm recollection he had of his teachers in the homage he pays them.

As for his instruction, Aldus might have had access to a printed copy of the Donatus grammar, the standard Latin schoolbook that was continuously passed on since the fourth century – it was the first book, in an edition of three hundred copies, from the Sweinheim and Pannartz press at Subiaco. But he would have almost certainly have had to compose his own copies of the classical Latin authors by writing down the readings and commentaries of his teacher. Very few of the teachers themselves would have owned their own manuscripts

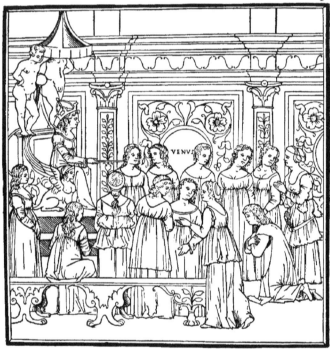

or books, and their texts derived from their own past instruc,
tors. The teacher was *il maestro* or master, who dictated

everything in Latin, drawing upon his own vast store of knowl/
edge of the classics, grammatical structure, etymology, biography,
geographical and historical allusions, mythology, philosophy
and moral appropriateness to doctrine with reference, perhaps,
to his own copied notes from other sources. All this storehouse
of encyclopedic matter was taken down by the students as they
composed their own books – the basic text of the author's work,
plus the commentary. Everything was subject, of course, to all
the errors inherent in hurried, poorly understood note/taking. It
may well have been at this point that the idea of making printed
books available in handy, inexpensive format could have occurred
to Aldus; for he was in the very city where the new art of printing
was first being practiced in Italy.

* *
*

SINCE 1467 when the German printers Sweinheim and
Pannartz left Subiaco, they had been publishing in Rome. In
the same year as their arrival, 1467, the first book was printed
in Rome.[20] There they had the patronage of the noble Massimo
family who, as humanists and patrons of the arts, welcomed
the pair to Palazzo Massimo in the heart of old Rome. The
University of Rome, known as the *Sapientia* from the inscrip/
tion over the entrance *(Initium sapientiae timor domini),* was
located in that same area near Piazza Navona that constituted
the heart of the city's intellectual and bookish life. Sweinheim
and Pannartz could not be better situated.

Sweinheim and Pannartz would later praise their Mas/
simo patrons, referring to them in the latinized humanist form
as "Maximus" to signify their support of the classics. In a

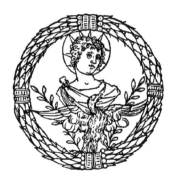

colophon, the two printers, defensive of their Germanic names — and perhaps remembering the invectives of Lorenzo Valla against the corruption of Latin by barbarous grammarians who seem to teach "gothically" while he defends the classical founts of language[21] — still manage to express their pride in their work: " If the reader wishes to learn the names of the workmen, let him read. He may laugh at the rough German names, but perchance the skill of the men may tone down the effect of words strange to the Muses. Masters Conrad Sweinheim and Arnold Pannartz have printed at Rome many such, and Petrus Maximus, together with his brother Franciscus, have provided a home suitable for the work."[22]

*

Another patron of the Sweinheim and Pannartz press was Cardinal Bessarion. Among the other books that issued from their press was the *editio princeps* of Bessarion's *In calumniatorem Platonis,* a vindication and defense of Plato against charges of immorality, which they printed in 1469. Many years later, in 1503, Aldus Manutius would reprint the cardinal's defense of Plato against his calumniators. It may have made an impression on him in his youth when he was in Rome, and he may have been acquainted with the Sweinheim and Pannartz publication. It is, according to Renouard, one of the rarest Aldine editions.

Bessarion's great collection of manuscripts and books was left to the Marciana Library in Venice and became the source for many of the texts that Aldus would eventually consult in order to ascertain the superior text for his own editions. It must have reminded him of his student days in Rome, and the infancy of printing in that city, to come across the Sweinheim and Pannartz volumes from Bessarion's library.

It can be conjectured, given his pursuit of classical studies in Rome, that Aldus would have been acquainted with the books from the Sweinheim and Pann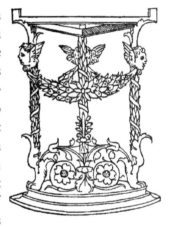artz press, which totaled fifty-two editions, including the first four at Subiaco done in a semi-Roman type, *caratteri sublacensi,* which is not to be seen again. Still extant is a trade list mentioning all of the printers' production: it was attached as a preface to a *Biblical Commentary* published in 1472 and addressed to Pope Sixtus IV.

Sweinheim and Pannartz continued their partnership in Rome until 1473, when they separated and Pannartz on his own issued another eleven books. By that time they no longer had a monopoly on printing. In 1470 an edition of Quintilian was published at an Italian-owned press in Rome; in 1471 the first book actually printed by an Italian, a priest named Clement of Padua, came out in Venice; and by 1475 the Italians had the new art well in hand and were asserting their own genius over it, being able by then to dispense with German workers. "Thus it was Italy where there originated the two kinds of type which have ever since been the basic elements of western printing, viz. 'roman' and 'italic'; which produced the first Greek and Hebrew fonts; where the title-page and pagination, music print and pocket edition were launched upon the world of letters."[23]

* *
*

VITAL TO ALDUS' formation as a scholar-publisher was his Roman sojourn, which imbued him with humanist ideals and classical education, and exposed him to the innovation of the printed book that could make texts available that had hitherto been well-guarded in private collections or made virtually inaccessible in monasteries. Later, as a publisher, Aldus would rail against hoarders who kept rare books to themselves. In his preface to the *Thesaurus cornucopiae* of 1496 he writes, "My only consolation is the assurance that my labors are helpful to all, and that the fame, and the use of my books increase from day to day, so that even the 'book-buriers'

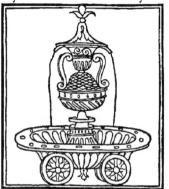

are now bringing their books out of their cellars and offering them for sale. This is just what I predicted years ago, when I was not able to get a single copy from anyone on loan, not even for one hour. Now I have got what I wanted: Greek volumes are made available to me from many sources....I do hope that, if there should be people of such spirit that they are against the sharing of literature as a common good, they may either burst of envy, become worn out in wretchedness, or hang themselves."

It is also the great achievement of Aldus that he managed to assimilate and transmit to succeeding generations the body of classical literature without getting caught up in factiousness. The humanists were often a vain bunch given to petty arguing and monstrous name-calling, invective and vituperation. They were the celebrities of their day, enjoying the company and adulation of princes and popes. What they did and said and whom among their company they attacked and reviled over petty grammatical differences or questions of pronunciation and other minutia, made the news of the day. Aldus was to remain a civil, humane exception.

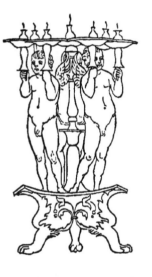

While our view of Roman humanism has become clearer in recent years,[24] Symonds' observation that it often flourished fitfully, precariously subject to the personal enthusiasms or restrictions of successive popes, retains some weight: "its growth being alternately checked and encouraged at the pleasure of the priest in office."[25] Nicholas V could put up with even the most scurrilous and anti-clerical invectives of Lorenzo Valla, but Pope Paul II, on the other hand, impatient with their pretensions and their alleged paganism, exercised his full wrath and authority over the humanists, accusing them of impiety. He suppressed the Roman Academy founded by

Giulio Pomponio and imprisoned him. He also imprisoned and tortured Platina, who was subsequently rehabilitated by Sixtus IV and appointed the first Vatican Librarian.

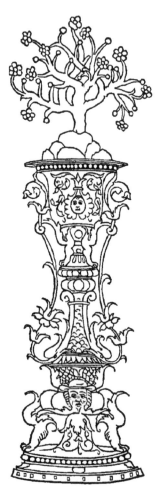

Aldus was in Rome during the pontificate of Paul II (1464-71), and he would have been aware of the various diatribes between the humanists and their changing fortunes under the popes, if only through his teacher, Gaspare da Verona, for it constituted the real matter of interest of his times. He would have undoubtedly absorbed the lessons of the precarious political climate – and its effect on what could or could not be printed – that obtained in the papal states. At some point in the 1470s, perhaps after the retirement of his teacher Gaspare da Verona in 1473, or even a few years later, since Domizio Calderini was lecturing until 1478, Aldus left Rome.

IV. ALDUS IN FERRARA AND CARPI

ALDUS LEFT ROME FOR FERRARA TO
continue his studies in Greek with Battista Guarini, the son
of an eminent pedagogue, Guarino de'Guarini, also known as
Guarino Veronese from the city of his birth, Verona. Ferrara,
situated between Venice and Bologna, was held as a duchy
by the powerful d'Este family and was a center of humanist
learning and literary development. But its preeminence as
a center for learning Greek dated back to the Councils of
Florence-Ferrara and the influx there of Greek scholars. During Aldus' residence in Ferrara in the mid or late 1470s, the
rule of Ercole I marked the apogee of the d'Este family. The
court was frequented by men of learning and artists and was
enlivened by Ercole's own well-instructed children. Isabella
d'Este, another pupil of Battista Guarini, may have come
to be acquainted with Aldus at this period, for she will later
become one of his correspondents and an assiduous purchaser
of his publications.

Mario Ferrigni, in his life of Aldus, speculates that Aldus
may have given lessons at the same time in which he was being
instructed in Greek by Guarini, and it may be at this time that
Aldus had as his pupil the future poet Ercole Strozzi, of the
noble Florentine family, whose work would later be published
in an Aldine edition. Most important of his friendships in Ferrara would be another pupil of Battista Guarini, the precocious
young Giovanni Pico della Mirandola (1463-94) who was to
encapsulate the brilliance of the age but perish young at the
height of his powers.

The Pico family were lords of Mirandola, but Giovanni renounced all his rights over the domain in order to dedicate himself completely to study. He was that prodigy of memory and intelligence whose name today is proverbial for insuperable mental capacity. He died at age thirty-one without being able to conclude the work towards which his studies tended – that is, examining all the philosophical systems known in his time to bring them to synthesis.

Already at age sixteen he had acquired enough "doc-trine" and wisdom to counsel his sister Caterina in the choice of tutor for her sons when they were left father-less by the premature death of Leonello Pio, lord of Carpi, an Emilian town not far from Mirandola. It was Giovanni Pico who recommended Aldus to his sister when her first son, Alberto, was four years old and the second, Leonello, still an infant.

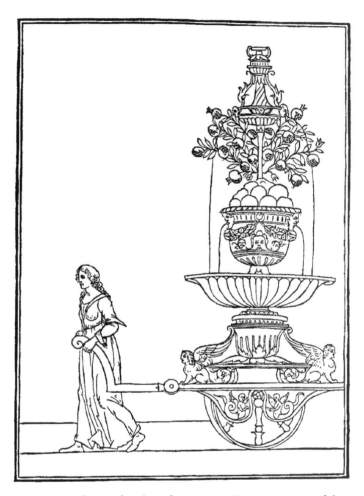

An erudite and cultured woman, Caterina accepted her brother's advice; and Aldus found employment at the Pio court, certainly a more modest one than that of Ferrara, under whose orbit were both Carpi and Mirandola, but an important move for Aldus' future. An alliance with a princely family or a university career was a means of livelihood and survival for scholars like Aldus.

* *

*

WHEN ALDUS ENTERED the employ of the Pio family and made his home in the castle at Carpi, the court and town were governed by Marco Pio as regent for his nephew Alberto. It was Marco Pio who, in a letter of March 18, 1480, conferred the citizenship of Carpi on Aldo Manuzio of Bassiano and had him exempt from taxes in recognition of the zeal with which he instructed Alberto Pio in grammar and literature. At that time Aldus bought a home in Carpi in the Sant'Antonio quarter.[27]

He would, however, have been frequently in the castle and a part of its life. The court of a small lord, like that of Carpi, was similar in its rhythm to the life of a great land-owner. Relatives, family adherents, in-laws, retainers, friends, clients, and servants all depended on the lord's protection and bounty. One can imagine the conflicting interests and attempts at attention and favor which flourished in such households. That Aldus was well regarded is documented both in correspondence and in the portrait of him that still exists in a mural painted on a chapel wall in the castle picturing Prince Pio with his familiars. One can still visit that castle of Carpi in the flat Emilian plains of central Italy where it commands the main town square, though there is no longer a moat or drawbridge to maintain its aloofness from the arcades opposite it.

In a preface to one of his eventual editions, Aldus will comment on his having educated Alberto and his young brother Leonello, right from the years "of their tiny fingernails" *(a teneris unguiculis).* From time to time, other young boys were also taught with the princes. One of Alberto Pio's companions in study was Jacopo Berengario who was given the privilege of being able to study with the prince and was to become a noted medical doctor and anatomist. It is possible to follow Aldus in his tutorial role since he has left singular testimony of this almost paternal duty in the ample letter addressed by him to Caterina Pio. The tone is somewhat that of a self-defense justification as if in reply to that lady's observation that Aldus seemed to be dedicating a lot of time to writing and composing rather than to instructing.

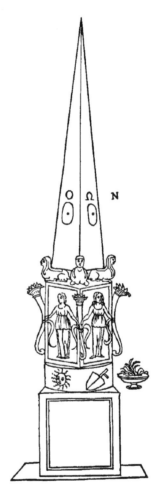

Aldus replies, "You know how near to my heart are your sons, entrusted to me so recently, and you can judge how much I occupy myself with them if you consider that I have had barely four hours a day to dedicate to my own work; a work I undertake not for my own use but in your service – that is, composing and writing a little grammar book particularly suited for instructing children. Another work I have undertaken on the accents, in order to teach them the correct pronunciation of words, without which knowledge it's impossible to progress further."[28]

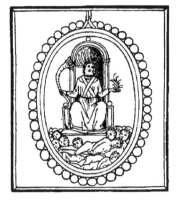

To bolster his argument with Caterina Pio about the necessity of his pupils learning Greek along with Latin, Aldus gives the examples of eminent Romans like Caesar and Cicero. If, he maintains, his pupils don't know Greek, how will they be able to have models of wisdom, eloquence, and virtue to imitate, as was the ideal of the time?

And he does compose these books and others, for this was the common task of tutors before printed books were widely obtainable, or, if obtainable, often unworthy as texts because of the many errors they con-tained. As if prenoting the future, Aldus presents his pupil with the book on accents on a New Year's Day when good resolu-tions are made, and he says, "begin with this...when you have learned it well, I will give you other more difficult books." In time he keeps his word by dedicating the first complete printed edition of Aristotle to his former pupil. It is a fitting gift for the former tutor to the then Prince Pio of Carpi – was not Aristotle himself tutor to Alexander the Great? Such classical allusions were expected between humanists.

It is not unlikely that from his own experiences as a student first in Rome, then in Ferrara, and later as a teacher Aldus became more and more convinced of the need that existed for good books in quantity. Even when manuscripts or early printed books existed, the textual variants were usually so great as to make the works misleading at best. Ferrigni believes that the *Rudimenta grammatices latinae linguae* written by Aldus and published in four editions is basically the work composed for the young princes, then revised and amplified.

* *
*

ALDUS WAS INDUCED by Giovanni Pico to visit Ferrara with the young Alberto so that his nephew could profit by mingling in those circles of humanists, poets, and courtiers that the city offered, and where, it seems, Alberto formed a friendship with Ercole Strozzi. They were there when the war between Venice and Ferrara broke out in 1482, and they fled for safety to Mirandola. In a future letter to the poet Poliziano, Aldus will recount his interval at Mirandola as an important time when he met various scholars.

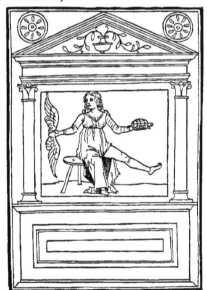

Aldus very likely spent the years between 1479 and 1488 in the employ of Caterina Pio. During those years he built up a circle of teachers, humanist colleagues, friends and acquaintances who will be remembered later in his dedications and prefaces.

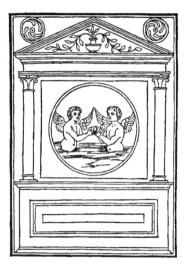

V. ALDUS AR⁓
RIVES IN VENICE

THE PERIOD FROM the time Aldus leaves Carpi in 1488 or 1489 for Venice, until he emerges in 1494 as a publisher, is hidden to all and subject to speculation. We know from his later prefaces that his goal in becoming a publisher was to issue correct texts in Greek and Latin of the classics. His complete im⁓ mersion in scholarly studies up to this point leads him unerringly to fulfill just such a goal and ambition. Yet, at almost forty years of age, it entails risk. It is a leap into the unknown from the security and protection of a small court where he was accepted as a family member, to the unknown trials and difficulties of setting up a press in the highly competitive Venice of that time.

Lamenting over and over again in his future prefaces
of the unremitting toil his life has become, it
seems that Aldus made his choice
because he could
do no less.

* * *
* *
*

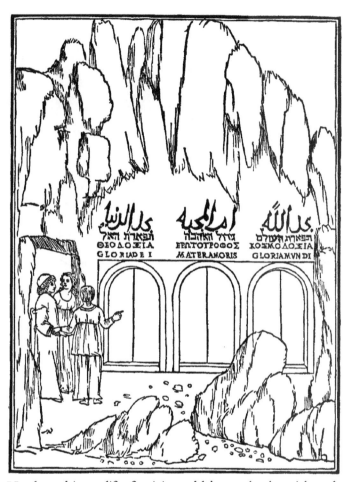

He plunged into a life of activity and labor so that he might real-
ize his desire of being, in his lifetime and after, of some use to all
people. It is a noble proposal and one in character with a man
who so often cited the example of Cato. In the humanist use of
finding a classical mentor, Aldus would come to be likened by

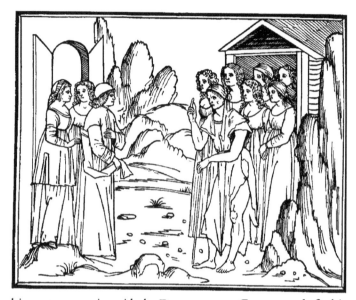

his contemporaries with the Roman censor Cato not only for his enduring admiration for Cato's zeal in learning Greek in his old age – an example he was often to cite in his prefaces – but also for his own rectitude, the austerity of his habits, his diligence and seriousness. Although his prefaces become filled with the litany of his arduous projects, his labor and toil, in one of them Aldus at least finds justification through the works of his ancient model: "Since, as Cato says, the life of a man is like that of iron which, if used, will wear out, but if unused rusts; thus man, if he is active, gets worn out, and if he isn't idleness will damage him more than all his labour." It is also in contrast to some of the other strong personalities contemporary with him who expressed themselves in violence, vanity, polemics, and scandal. Aldus is an antidote to a Caesar Borgia, a Pope Paul II, or even the humanist Lorenzo

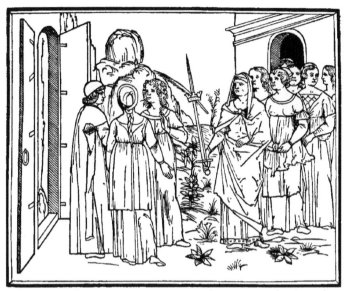

Valla whose learning was not put to the service of others, but rather to advance his own feeling of superiority over them.

Even the elder Guarini, as tutor of the young Lionello d'Este at the ducal court in Ferrara, had entered into a typical humanist's duel with Poggio Bracciolini over the respective merits of Scipio Africanus and Julius Caesar.[29] Poggio preferred the character of Scipio; Guarino, to curry favor with his pupil Lionello of the powerful d'Este house who admired Caesar, defended the latter by throwing contempt on Poggio. So the humanist aspiration to return to the classics for moral guidance and examples of noble living often deteriorated into bitter partisan feuds as senseless as they were prolonged. It was an arena that Aldus never entered.

About five years of needed preparation in which to learn the techniques of the new art separate the documented account of

Aldus' life at Carpi until his emergence as a publisher in Venice. Five years in which to procure source material and establish by collation and philological study the soundest texts. He made printing not just a faster means of copying past mistakes, but a scholarly achievement of presenting the best text as culled from comparative studies. For such an undertaking he had to provide the best type, obtain collaborators of high calibre, and raise money to purchase equipment and to begin.

*　*

*

LIFE FOR ALDUS – his life of fame – starts when he is past forty. What he wrought, from the appearance of his first published book in 1493 until his death in 1515, was something akin to the first editorial boom. He launched his namesake Aldine editions of the classics in an economical, pocket-sized, scholarly, and impeccable series. He made the book an accessible vehicle of thought and communication.

Aldus' arrival in Venice is probably sometime around 1488, based on what he, as Aldus Manutius Basianas Romanus, indicates in a preface to the *Thesaurus cornucopiae* published "with the greatest care and enormous effort" in August 1496. Addressing himself "to all students," he writes, "in our day it is indeed a difficult task for the friend of good literature to print Latin books correctly. It is even harder to print Greek books, and the hardest of all tasks is to print in both languages without mistakes. You know the great care I am taking to have those books printed in spite of all difficulties, and as expeditiously as possible. Ever since I started this enterprise *seven years ago* I have not had a single quiet hour, this I can swear."[30]

Why did Aldus leave Carpi where he might have started his press with the help of the Pio family? Aldus must certainly have realized the advantages that he would have in Venice, which was then the greatest commercial center of Europe and the pivot of an established network of trade routes. Capital was readily available there for the establishment of presses, as already evidenced by the boom in printing. Even more important,

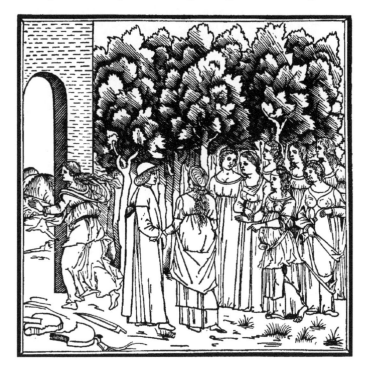

perhaps, was the concentration of Greek scholars in Venice who would be essential to Aldus' goal of bringing into print all of the Greek classics, as well as those in Latin. From the

Greeks who had thronged to Venice after the fall of Constantinople to the Turks in 1453, Aldus would draw his collaborators,

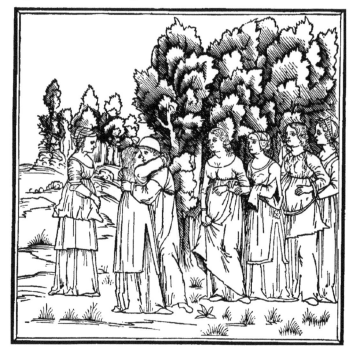

from proofreaders to editors. Aldus was also aware that Venice
possessed possibly the best collection of Greek manuscripts in
all Italy, donated to the Serene Republic by Cardinal Bessarion
and deposited in the Marciana Library. And perhaps it was also
the recollection of his early years in Rome, when Pope Paul II
dealt so harshly with humanists, that persuaded Aldus that
the tolerant and lenient climate of the Adriatic republic was
more conducive to the publishing business than the restrictions
prevailing elsewhere.

IN VENICE Aldus, a novice to the printing trade, would find typographers and workmen now familiar with the craft. After the initial exclusive privilege for printing granted to John of Speyer, the Venetian Senate astutely recognized the importance of the new invention and decreed that it would be welcomed and assisted in Venice. The republic wanted to attract publishers and encourage printing as an important staple of business and commerce, and the city on the lagoon proved an ideal place for the practice and spread of printing. There was a notable influx of German printers after John of Speyer, including Erhard Ratdolt, Franz Renner, and Christopher Valdarfer.

HUMANISM HAD DEVELOPED A THIRST FOR LEARNING THAT COULD ONLY BE SATIATED BY THE RAPID PRODUCTION OF BOOKS THUS SUSTAINING MANY PRESSES; AND WEALTHY PATRONS ABOUNDED IN THE FLOURISHING CITY.

VEN BEFORE THE INVENTION of movable type, Venice, like the Low Countries and Germany, had been a center for imprinting on wooden tablets and wood-cuts – a production that specialized in the Donatus for students, psalters, and playing cards.

But only about fifteen years after the first published books issued from Mainz, in 1470 one of the most celebrated of all typographers, the Frenchman Nicholas Jenson, arrived in Venice and proceeded to cut a roman typeface of great beauty. He must have recognized its perfection, for he never cut any other font of roman. Jenson printed from 1470 to 1480 and produced 155 identified books. He was much honored in his lifetime, being created Count Palatine by Pope Sixtus IV, and he left a will that shows that his printing brought him not only fame and glory but wealth, as well. In the decade when Jenson printed, Venetian publications in general reached a peak of excellence that was not to be realized again until Aldus began printing. Although

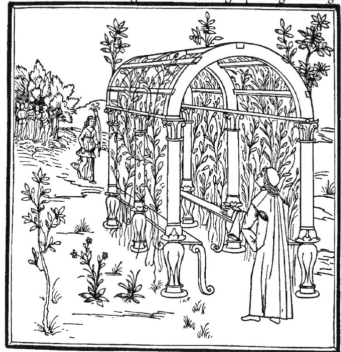

the overall standard of printing declined after 1480, Venice as a book market was thriving on the production of its presses.

There is a document conserved in the Marciana Library known by its Venetian name, *Zornale,* or journal, an abstract of which is reprinted in Horatio Brown's historical study of the Venetian printing press.[31] This oblong ledger is the authentic record-book of a Venetian bookseller in which, day by day, from May 17, 1484 until October 1485, are recorded the names of books sold, the prices paid, and in some cases the names of purchasers. Although it is meant to be only an impersonal inventory of stock, it becomes an extraordinarily human document, for it provides direct insight into the reading tastes of the times and an idea of how the book-seller plied his trade. This particular book-seller, unknown by name, bought books from the printer-publisher for cash and usually sold them for cash to the public at large. In some instances, however, it can be seen by his notations that he used his book stock to pay for services, for example, one hundred copies of a novel to the binder, a Bible to the proofreader, and Cicero's *Orations* in exchange for wine.

The bookseller listed the books with which he started his business and the number of copies of each that were still in stock. His total inventory on May 17, 1484 was the respectable number of 1,337 volumes; and it can be ascertained from his list which were some of the more popular works. The bookseller had on hand eight copies of Isidore of Seville's *Etymologiae* (an encyclopedic work that transmitted to medieval and Renaissance scholars a good deal of classical learning), thirteen copies of *Peregrinatio ad Jerusalem (A Pilgrimage to Jerusalem),* ten copies each of Donatus and Juvenal, and many copies of various devotional works. On May 31, *Peregrinatio* and Juvenal were sold out and Donatus was running low.

From the number of copies sold and prices obtained for certain editions, it can be ascertained that some printer-publishers were in special repute, and their editions are identified. The bookseller carried a variety of stock: the classics, bibles, missals, canon law, breviaries, romances, school books, poetry. Prices varied according to the work, from a mere nine soldi for Poggio's *Facetiae* to three gold ducats, four lire and eighteen soldi for an illustrated Ptolemy. A good bit of the bookseller's stock was in the gold ducat bracket and could not have been so easily acquired by students, impecunious scholars, or the public at large.

*

ALDUS must have spent his first years in Venice acquainting himself with the book market, with the printing process, with the whole exhilarating scene of book learning and production, perhaps also continuing to tutor pupils in Latin and Greek as he learned his new trade. As is true of much of his life, the early Venetian years of Aldus Manutius are shrouded in mystery, and it cannot be said with certainty whether he worked alone or with someone, or if he used his own funds or was subsidized.

From a relatively obscure tutor, he began to be known as a Hellenist scholar in humanist circles as his correspondence shows. Sometime between 1488 and 1491 Aldus had his own writings, known as the *Musarum panagyris,* containing among the components his letter to Caterina Pio, printed as a pamphlet by Baptista de Tortis, an industrious printer who published 180 books between 1480 and 1500. Aldus' publication of this work falls between 1487 and 1491.

* * *
* *
*

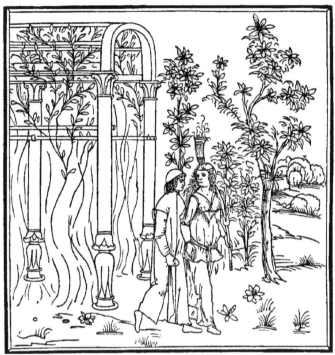

It was undertaken perhaps for the purpose of acquiring some familiarity with the printing process, or perhaps even some advance notice before he himself entered the highly competitive business of book publishing.[32] More importantly, in 1493 Aldus had his Latin grammar published by Andrea Torresani who had his press in the San Paternian quarter. In its preface, Aldus announced his plan for going on to publish a Greek grammar and other works. The establishment of Aldus' connection with an experienced printer and successful businessman like Andrea Torresani might have been the conclusive step that led him to begin his own press.

ANDREA TORRESANI, ALSO KNOWN AS
ANDREA D'ASOLA FROM HIS BIRTHPLACE,
WAS BORN IN 1451, JUST A YEAR AFTER AL-
DUS, AND LEFT ASOLA IN THE VENETIAN
TERRITORIES NEAR MANTUA AT THE AGE
OF TWENTY. HE WENT TO VENICE, WHERE
HE WAS CAUGHT UP WITH THE NEW ART OF
PRINTING, AND BECAME A WORKMAN AT
JENSON'S PRESS.

FTER JENSON'S DEATH IN 1480,
Andrea bought Jenson's type and took over the printing
establishment, running it successfully and producing
mainly law books to supply the demand of Venetian
counsels and students at the University of Padua. In a petition dated
June 2, 1524, Andrea Torresani mentions his fiftieth anniversary
as a printer, thus dating his beginning in that field as 1474.[33] Not
learned, but a businessman by instinct and training, Andrea was
deeply experienced in the new book-printing trade as he had
learned it from working with a master like Jenson. He would
be the very man that Aldus needed, providing the right balance
of business practicality to Aldus' scholarly bent.

Torresani printed the first edition of Sabellico's *Storia di
Venezia,* which was dear to the Venetian Senate and accorded
the first known author's copyright. When Aldus arrived in
Venice and prepared himself for his printing venture, he was
most likely to have met Andrea Torresani. It may well be that the
very first Aldine editions, which bear no mention of where they
were printed, came from Torresani's press.

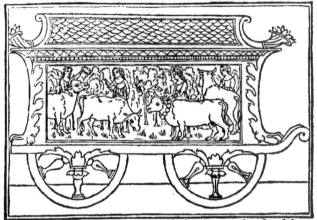

Quella Nympha cófifa la finiſtra tabula cótineua, che afcenſo hauea
fopra il manſueto & candido Tauro. Et quello q̊lla p el tumido mare ti
mida, tráſſretaua.   SECVNDA SINISTRA.

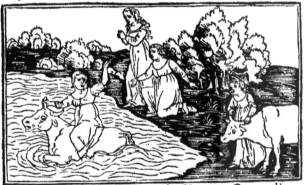

Nel fronte anteriore, Cupidine uidi cū inumera Caterua di promi
ſcua géte uulnerata, mirabódi che egli tiraſſe larco ſuo uerſo lalto olym
po. In nel fronte poſteriore, Marte mirai dinanti al throno del magno
Ioue, Lamentátiſe che el filiolo la ipenetrabile thoraca ſua egli la haueſ-
ſe lacerata. Et el benigno ſignore el ſuo uulnerato peċto gli monſtraua.
Et nellaltra mano extenſo el brachio teniua ſcripto,   NEMO.

                                              k   iiii

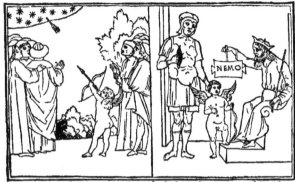

Quefta figura di carro era q̃drāgula di dui q̃drati pfeɛ̃ti p lōgo di pedi
.vi.alto.iiii.lato altrotāto cū exigēte coronice di fopra & di fotto el plin⸗
tho, Et da q̃ ífopra uno & femipedi era una plana lata pedi dui & femi,
lōga. v. & femi, cū uno pclinato uerfo la coronice tutto fquāmeo de pre⸗
tiofiffime petre, cum alterato congreffo & ordine di coloramento Et ne
gli quatro anguli erano appaɛ̃te copie inuerfe cum lapertura refupina,
fopra el proieɛ̃to angulare della coronice, ſtipata di molti fruɛ̃ti & fiori
de craffe & multiplice gemme germināte tra la uariata fogliatura doro.
Gliquali corni uidi cum egregia expreffione di folie di papauero cor⸗
nuto, inueſtiti & di alueoli intorquati, & cum il fuo gracilamento inuo⸗
luto al termine della plana. Ilquale fi rūpeua í uno folio laciniato antiq̃
rio, che belliffimamente deriuaua fopra el dorfo della elegante copia del
la materia diɛ̃ta. In ciafcūo angulo dal plintho uerfo la coronice, al pro
ieɛ̃to era affermato, uno Harpyiatico pede, cum moderato finuare, & cū
præſtante conuerfione de qui & delli infoliamento di Acantho.

Le rote erano teɛ̃te intro nel carro, La medietate fua apparēdo, Et el
plintho cioe la extrema parte di effa machina, nellanteriore parte, proxí
mo ad gli harpatici pedi, alquāto fubleuantife politamente gracilifcēte
uertiuafe in uno limachale uoluto. Nelquale erano gli laquei, o uero re
tinaculi ad trahere opportunamente commēdati. Et oue infixo uertiua
laxide, ad effo plintho appaɛ̃to pendeua uno mucronato, di tanta latitu
dine alla iunɛ̃tura del plintho, quāto era due fiate dal uolubile meditu⸗
lo alla cima. Et quiui exquifitamente principiauano due foliature, Le⸗
quale diuidentefe fotto el plintho deriuauano, Nel medio della difcre⸗
pantia delle quale promineua modificamēte una pētaphylla rofa, nel
mediano

mediano dellaquale uertiuafe effo polo nellaxide. Come appare nella tabella prima.

Hora fopra la plana antedicta iaceua uno fatale candidiffimo & benigno Tauro, de molti fiori adornato, & di pompa di boue libabondo. Sopra gli fedeua una regia uirgine degli ampli tergori, Cum gli longi, & nudi brachii, quafi ifpagurita tenendofe gli peduli palearii amplexaua. Induta exquifitiffimamente di panno fubtile, de feta uerde & de oro, de mirauegliofa textura, di habito Nympheo, cu le extremitate, di uno uelamine confine alle tatule fuccinctulo, uelificante, no fenza copia di ua rii gioielli exornata, cum una corona doro, fupprimente una elegantiffima & aurea cæfarie, mundula prænitente.

Quefto tale triumpho traheuano fei lafciui centauri figlioli dil caduco feme dillaudace Ifione. Cum piane cathenule doro agli robufti & equini fianchi exquifitamente illaqueate, Cum gli anuli luno cum laltro fuppreffamente innodantife, & retinute nelle auree fibule & connexi, & pofcia in le appacte armille difcorrendo al tirare æqualmente tutti fei. Ne fimigliante modo Erichthonio nel coiungere degli feroci cabal li alle uolucre quadrige ritrouoe.

Ciafcuno equitaua una ifigne Nympha, fedente cum le fpalle luna alaltra riuoltate, tre cum le fpectatiffime facie alla dextera couerfe, & tre alla parte leua, Cum inftrumenti muficali infeme cæleftemente di harmonia participati, cum uberrima & flaua capillatura, giu per gli candi di colli diftente, Cum pancarpie ornata la fua tefta, Veftite due proxime al triumpho di feta Cyanea, quale luculeo & eximio coloramento dille plumule nel collo del Pauone.

Le due mediane di folgorante Chermeo. Et le prime præcedente de panno rafo di coloratione Smaragdinea uerdigiante. Non fencia gli Nymphali additamenti, & decoramini, cantante cum le ritondate buccule, & cum tanta fuauitate fonante, di melodia, di conferuare impafta lalma fempre uiua.

Gli Centauri di Dendrocyfto coronati. Ne le mano fue, la una alla parte ima, & cum laltra amplexando geftauano gli dui propinqui al carro, uafi di antiquario expreffo, di Topacio di Arabia, cum el fuo fulgente colore aureo, grato a Lucina, & alquale le onde fe quiefcono. Negli fui fundi gracili, & nel mediano immoderata corpulentia paulatine augentife, Et dindi pofcia uerfo lorificio faftigiantife di altitudine bipedale, fencia anfule de miro artificio. Fora degliquali pfiliua uno nebulate fumo de fragratia tropo iextimabile fpargeti. Gli fequeti fona uao tube doro, cu pedete pano fericeo fubtile, di aureo itexto, cu tripli-

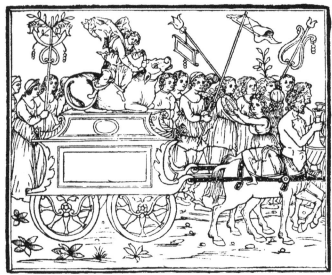

ce ligatura alla fiſtula tubale, Gli altri dui cū ueterrimi cornitibici concordi ciaſcuno & cum gli inſtrumenti delle Equitante nymphe.

Sotto lequale triúphale ſeiughe era laxide nel meditullo , Nelq́le gli
rotali radii erano infixi , deliniamento Baluſtico ,graciliſcenti ſepoſa
negli mucronati labii cum uno pomulo alla circunferentia. Elquale
Polo era di finiſſimo & ponderoſo oro,repudiante el rodicabile erugi-
ne,& lo incédioſo Vulcano,della uirtute & pace exitiale ueneno. Sum-
mamente dagli feſtigianti celebrato,cum moderate , & repentine
riuolutióe intorno ſaltanti,cum ſolemniſſimi plauſi , cum
gli habiti cinĉti di faſceole uolitante, Et le ſedente ſopra gli trahenti centauri. La Sanĉta cagione,
& diuino myſterio,inuoce cõſone & car-
mini cancionali cum extre
ma exultatione amo-
roſamente lauda
uano.
**
*

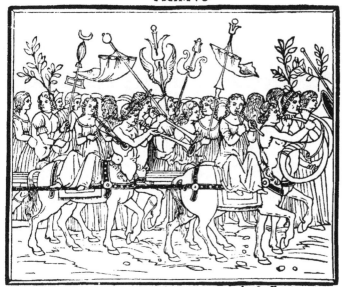

EL SEQVENTE triúpho nú meno mirauegliofo dl primo. Impo
che egli hauea le qtro uolubile rote tutte, & gli radii, & il meditullo defu
fco achate, di cádide uéule uagaméte uaricato. Ne tale certamte geftoe re
Pyrrho cú le noue Mufe & Apolline i medio pulfáte dalla natura ípffo.

Laxide & la forma del dicto qle el primo, ma le tabelle erão di cyaneo
Saphyro orientale, atomato de fcintillule doro, alla magica gratiffimo,
& longo acceptiffimo a cupidine nella finiftra mano.

Nella tabella dextra mirai exfcalpto una infigne Matróa che
dui oui hauea parturito, in uno cubile regio colloca
ta, di uno mirabile pallacio, Cum obftetrice ftu
pefacte, & multe altre matrone & aftante
NympheDegli quali ufciua de
uno una flammula, & delal-
tro ouo due fpectatiffi
me ftelle.

* *

r.

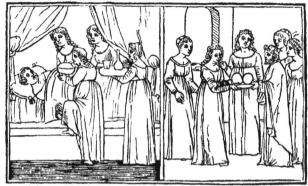

Nellaltra affula gli curiofi parenti del nouo prodigio ignari, Nel
Apollineo templo al diuo Simulachro per oraculo, la caufa & lo exito
diuoti interrogauano. Agliquali el benigno Nume cufi perplexibel-
mente gli refpondeua. Vni gratum mare. Alterum gratum mari. Per tale ambiguo refponfo dagli pii parenti furono referuati.

TABELLA SINISTRA.

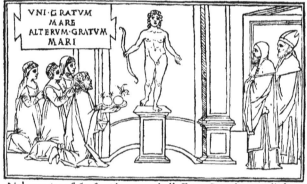

Nel anteriore frôte fe uideua uno bellifftimo Cupidine puellulo, nel
æthera leuato, & cum el ftrale tagliente di una aurea fagitta, nel ftellife-
ro cælo, uarie figure di animali quadrupedi, reptili, & uolatili uiolente-
mente dipingere, Et in terra mirabondi gli humani ftauano, per tanto
effecto di una fragile fagittula. In nel pofteriore, el magno Iupiter, uno
folerte paftore, in fuo loco iudice collocaua, excitato da effo ꝓximo ad

uno lepidiſſimo fonte dormiente. Oue a tre nude & formoſiſſime Dee, faceua iudicio. Elquale dal operoſo Cupidine ſeducto, allaſua facetiſſima genitrice el pomo conſentiua.

PARS ANTERIOR ET POSTERIOR.

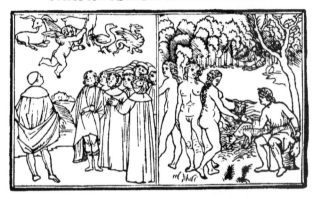

Queſto triumphale carro ſeni Elephanti candidi, binati iuncti, qua li non ſi.ritrouerebbeno nella Ageſinua patria, ne agli gandari, Ne tali furono ſubiugati al Triumpho africo del magno Pompeo, Ne tali furono ad trahere el Triumpho de Libero Patre lindia uicta, cum el proboſcide armato de gli eburnei & exitiali denti, & cum ſuaue barrito acconciamente traheuano, cum retinaculi de finiſſima ſeta di tinctura Cyanea, intorta belliſſimamente cum fili doro, & de argentei commixti, inſtrictiſſimi nodi ſpicatamente textili quadrangulari, Quale ſe uideno le ſpiche del monte Gargano, cum pectorali aurei di multitudine di fulgentiſſime & diſſentanee gemme referti, cum armille auree appacte, nellequale diſcorreuano a tutti ſei la uinculatura. Sei tenerime fanciulle ancora æquitauano al modo delle prime, cum altri diſſimili inſtrumenti, in uno ſono optimamente comparticipati, Et tuto quello che le altre faceano, & queſte el ſimigliante. Veſtite due di Phœniceo, Due di prænitente luteo, quale colore interno del flore del Apio Ranino, & due di uiolacea purpura, Contecti gli uehiculari Ele phanti erano de copertura doro infimbriata di craſſe perle, & de altre gemme pompoſamente decorati. Et el collo circundato de rotondi & craſſi gioielli, Et ſopra lamplo fronte dependeua uno inſtabile pomulo di mirabile perle, cũ una prolixa barbula di uaria ſeta & fili aurei al moto inconſtante.

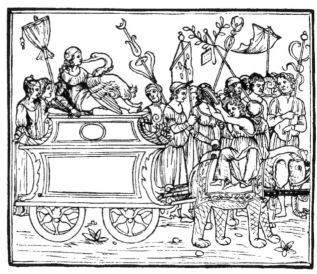

Sopra de quefto fuperbo & Triumphale uectabulo, uidi uno bianchiffimo Cycno, negli amorofi amplexi duna inclyta Nympha filiola
de Thefeo, dincredibile bellecia formata, & cum el diuino roftro obfcu
lantife, demiffe le ale, tegeua le parte denudate della igenua Hera, Et cu
diuini & uoluptici obletamenti iftauano delettabilmente iucundiffimi ambi connexi, Et el diuino Olore tra le delicate & niuee coxe collocato. Laquale commodamente fedeua fopra dui Puluini di panno doro, exquifitamente di mollicula lanugine tomentati, cum tutti gli fumptuofi & ornanti correlarii opportuni. Et ella induta de uefta Nympha
le fubtile, de ferico bianchiffimo cum trama doro texto præluccente
Agli loci competenti elegante ornato de petre pretiofe.
Sencia defecto de qualunque cofa che ad incremen-
to di dilecto uenuftamente concorre. Summa
mente agli intuenti confpicuo & dele
ctabile. Cum tutte le parte che
al primo fue defcripto
di laude & plau
fo.
*

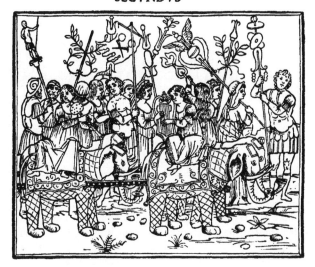

EL TERTIO cæleste triumpho feguiua cum quatro uertibile rote di Chryſolitho æthiopico fcintule doro flammigiante, Traiecta per el-quale la feta del Aſello gli maligni dæmonii fuga, Alla leua mano gra-to, cum tutto quello c̄ di ſopra di rote e dicto. Dapoſcia le aſſule fue in ambito per el modo compacte ſopra narrato, erano di uirente Helitro-pia Cyprico, cum potere negli lumi cæleſti, el fuo geſtāte cœla, & il diui-nare dona, di ſanguinee guttule punctulato.

Offeriua tale hiſtoriato inſculpto la tabella dextra. Vno homo di re-gia maieſtate iſigne, Oraua in uno ſacro templo el diuo ſimulacro, quel lo che della formoſiſſima fiola deueua ſeguire. Sentendo el patre la eie-ctione ſua per ella del regno. Et ne per alcuno fuſſe pregna, Fece una munita ſtructura di una excelſa torre, Et in quella cum ſoléne cuſtodia la fece inclauſtrare. Nella qua-le ella ceſſabonda aſſedédo, cum ex-ceſſiuo ſolatio, nel uirgi neo ſino gutte do ro ſtillare uede ·ua.

✳

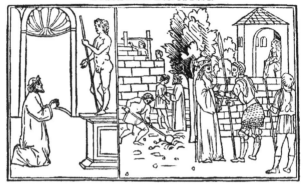

Nelaltra tabella era impreſſo uno nobile giouene. Ilquale cum ſum
ma religione receueua una protectióe di uno cryſtallino clypeo, Et egli
ualoroſo cum la falcata & tagliente Harpe,una terrifica donna decapita
ua,& el trunco capo inſigno di uictoria ſuperbaméte geſtaua. Del cruo‑
re delquale,naſceua uno alato caballo,che uolando in uno faſtigio di
monte,una myſterioſa fontana,cum il calce faceua ſurgente.

SECVNDA SINISTRA.

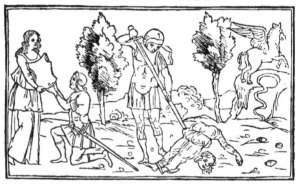

Nella facia anteriore uedeuaſi el potente Cupidine che cũ laurea ſa‑
gitta ſua uerſo li ſtelliferi cæli trahédo gutte doro amoroſamente faceua
pioucre. Et una iſinita turba di omni conditione uulnerata ſtauano di‑
cio tutti ſtupefacti. In oppoſito,uidi Venere irabonda,ſoluta cũ uno ar
migero da uno fatale rete el filiolo per le ale préſo hauea uindicabonda,
&uoleualo

& uoleualo difpénare,hauendo gia pieno el pugno delle,uolante plu-
mule,& il fanciullo piangendo, Vno cum gli talari mádato dallexcelfo
Ioue,fopradi uno throno fedéte,dalle forcie materne illæfo lo liberaua.
Et pofcia cufi ad qllo lofferiua . Et lo opitulo Iupiter gli diceua i atthica
lingua fculpto egregiaméte di rincontro della diuina bucca. ΣΥΜΟΙ-
ΓΛΥΚΥΣΤΕΚΑΙ ΓΙΚΡΟΣ.& copriualo fotto el fuo cæleste chlamyde
PARS ANTERIOR ET POSTERIOR.

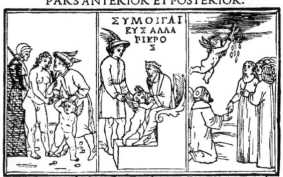

Quefto pompofaméte traheuano fei atrociffimi monoceri,cú la cor
nigera fronte ceruina,alla gelida Diana riuerenti. Gli quali in uincula-
ti erano al uigorofo &equino pecto,in uno ornaméto doro copiofo de
pretiofiffime gioie,cú funiculi intorti de filatura argentea & di lutea feta
lo uno cú laltro artificiofaméte inodantifi,politiffimi nodi faceano, cú
gli præftanti accefforii degliantifcripti.Sei uirguncule al modo & pom
pa de le altre fopra fedeuano,& cú habito doro intramato di finiffima fe
ta Cyanea,in uarii flori & frondatura itexti,tutte fei cum mirabili & ueterrimi iftrumenti da flato concordi,& cú incredibili fpiriti expreffi.So
pra la plana delquale nel medio iaceua uno pretiofo fcáno di uerdegiá-
te Iafpide,præftabile in argéto,officiofo al parto,&al cafto medicina.Il-
quale nel pede era exangulo, opportunaméte afcendendo gracile fotto
una cóchula platinata.La parte ima dellaquale fina al mediano fuo ope
rofamente fulcata.Et pofcia fchietta finuata fina fotto allabio nextrula-
to.La lacuna dellaquale poco profunda,al cómodo del fedéte,cum no-
tabili liniaméti itagliatura.Sopra qfto promptamente fedeua una orna
tiffima Nympha & belliffima iueftito aureo itexto cú feta cyanea,i habi
to fubtile di puellitia politura di multiplice géme deoinato.Indicaua el
fuo affectuofo dilecto,p mirare nel fuo gremio una copia di cæleste oro.
cú li foléni honori &gaudiofi applaufi qleglialtri,fedeua cú le ubere co
me p el dorfo effufe,coróata de diademate aureo& di multi formi lapilli.

l

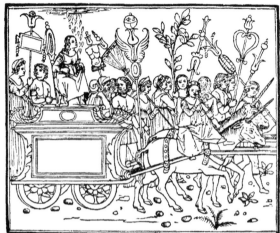

EL QVARTO triúpho q̃tro rote el portauáo di ferrineo A ſueſto
archado una fiata accéſo renuéte la extíctióe. Il reſiduo di tabulatura q̃-
drágula, cú il mó añdicto, era di folgoráte carbúculo tragoditáo , nó te-
médo le déſe tenebre, di expolitiſſime cælature, longo di ragionaméto
diſtinctaméte. Ma quale operature cóſiderare ſi douerebe in quale loco ,
& da quale artiſice furono fabricate.

Dúq̃ la dextera facia optimam̃te tale dimóſtraua hiſtoria. Vna uiene
rabile matróa p̃gnáte. Allaq̃le el ſúmo Iupiter diuinam̃te(q̃le cú la Dea
Iunone ſole)cú tonitri & fulmini li appeua,itáto che accéſa ſe cremaua
incinere,& del cóbuſto, uno nobiliſſimo & diuo iſantulo extraheuano.

TABELLA DEXTRA.

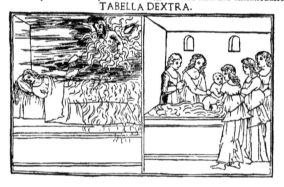

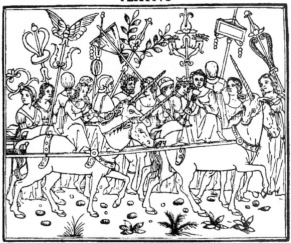

Nelaltra io mirai eſſo opitulatore Iupiter,q̃llo medeſimo infantulo, ad uno cæleſte homo talaricato & caduciſero gli oſſeriua. Et q̃ſto poſcia in uno antro a multe Nymphe nutriendo el commendaua.

SECVNDA SINISTRA.

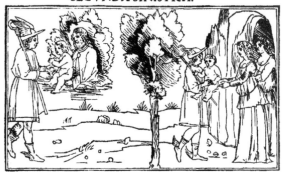

Nello q̃drato anteriore uidi Cupidie,mirauegliãtiſi grãde Copia di oi ſexo ſagittati,che cũ la ſua noxia ſagittula tirata nel alto cœlo Ioue tra heſſe in diuinitate ad cõtéplatióe d una mortale fanciulla. Allincõtro re tro el maxío Iupiter uedeuaſi í uno tribunale ſedéte iudice, Et cupidine claudicáte,cótra la ſua benigna matre i iudicio uocata,doléte q̃rimonie

faceua,Cóciofia cofa che p fua cagióe dellamore duna fpeciofiffima da‑
migella extremamente fe medefimo uulneraffe. Et che da una lucernale
fcintilla gli fuffe ftata la diuina gábula caufticata.Præfente ancora la bel
liffima Nympha cum la lucerna nelle mano accufata.Et a Cupidine ri‑
dibódo gli diceua Iupiter.Perfer fcintillá,qui cælú accendis & omnes.

PARS ANTERIOR ET POSTERIOR.

PERFER·SCINTILAM
QVI CAELVM· ACCEN
DIS·ET·OMNES

Queſto monoſtichó era efcalpto di formule noſtrate i una abaca tabel
la icófpecto della facia ðl uenerádo Nume.Il refiduo come li defcripti.
Queſto myſteriofo triúpho,fei maculofe,cú notule de fuluo nitente, &
uelociffime di pnicitate Tigride di Hyrcania illa ҩate belliffimaméte cú
flexibile palmite di fœconda uite, piene di tenere fróde, cú gli uolubili
Capreoli,ornate di uermigliacei corymbi.Nel trahere cú tépato moto.
    Di fopra elҩle nel mediáo ðella plana,era fituata una Bafi doro, p dia
metro iſimo pede uno & palmi.iii.alta il fimile pximo.Vna pte allo iſi‑
mo lataſtro rotódato,& femiſſo allundula,o uero refupina fima & nex‑
trulo.Il refiduo era diſtributo alla Trochlea, & alla iuerfa undula cú gli
acceſſorii nextruli,o uero reguli & cordicelle.La plana di ҩſta era nel me
diáo circulareméte uacua.Nella ҩle excauatióe defcédeuáo le caude di
ҩtro Aҩle,fúdate fopra la fupficie planata della bafi.Leҩle erão de ptio‑
fo Aetite puniceo di Perfia.Et ҩſte cú el dorfo ſtauano una alaltra oppo
fita.hauédo le ungiute bráchie doro ifixe calcante fopra la dicta bafi. Et
ciafcúa ambe le ale leuate cohæréte.Sopra de ҩſte nel cubito era fundato
ҩto mirádo uafo di æthiopico hyacitho lucidiffimo,& inimico del cel
te,comite gratiofo.Elҩle uafo era cruſtato di fmaragdo,cú multiplice al
tre uenule di géme,cofa icredibile.De altecia era femiſſo & pedi.ii.Qua
fi di forma ritódata.Il diametro dellaҩle fua craſſitudine,pſtauafi di uno
pede & femi,& la circúferétia cóſtaua tre diametri.Ilҩle uafo dal imo fo‑
pra le ale affirmato faliua triéte, & pofcia era uno frigio ambiéte lultima
craſſiiudine

craffitudie di uno palmo. dalq̃le phrygio, final pricipio duno uafo gut
turnio che fe coteniua i uno cũ q̃fto medefimo uno palmo, i fuma fina
qui eglie uno pede e medio. Sopra qfta diméfione nafceua una forma di
uafo fopra dicto leuato uno pede, & dilatarfe icominciaua fina uno pal
mo & femiffo. Ilq̃le femiffo, era diftribu to allexqfito phrygio di iuolute
fróde & flori q̃fi tutti euulfi deeffo hyacintho. Il diametro dui q̃rti et me
dio. Sotto q̃fto phrygietto pmieuáo icircuito alcúe fcidule di modefto
leuaméto & téperato carinato, alq̃to nel fupmo craffe, & nel fundo gra-
cilifcéte fe pdeuáo. Belliffimamte pofcia afcédeua fina alorificio dui q̃r-
ti & femi. Lacunato egregiamete di itorquate lacunule. Lorificio di una
cóchula cũ gli oruli lata, di feta la corpulétia cũ elegáte fima, & nella có
prehéfa del uafo, cũ tornatile gulule undule & toreti, Di tali liniamenti
eráo ifepti & de fotto & de fopra gli phrygii. Al phrygio dl gutturnio de
fotto nel dicto fepto fe coteniua dui mutilati conduli, o uero femi anuli,
fupp̃ffi dilla fua figura ptranfuerfo oppofiti cũ ladúcitate luno allaltro.
Gliq̃li nelle mordice fauce de due lacerte, o uero Dracoculi erano tenu
ti. Et gli Dracoculi de uena de fmaragdo pfectemete relicti, el refiduo de
cruftato, laceuano cũ q̃tro lacertacei pediculi fopra el culmo del uafo i-
feriore elq̃le culmo, tra el gutturnio, & lo iferiore uafo, la fua eminentia
era uno q̃rto. Et dal fublime gracilaméto fuo, defcédendo terminaua cũ
liniaméto de iuerfa fima al circúferito lymbo della corpulentia, oue era
lábiéte phrygio. Ilq̃le accliuato culmo era diligétiffimaméte fquámato
del hyacintho. Relicti folamete della fmaragdina uena gli Draconculi,
cũ el ferpéte uétre fopra el fquámato retinuto, & cufi gli q̃tro pediculi.
Gliq̃li dracoculi luno p lato al fine icifo del plapfo del dicto culmo, fopra lincifo della coronicetta, cũ la iuertifcéte cauda uerfo la fpina faceua
no una circulare & pmpta fpira. Et pofcia ne faceuáo uno altro fimile di
fotto. Quefti uoluti eráo p le anfe. Il uertigine iferiore, oue era cũ el uafo
cóiúcto, fecto i due pte una de q & laltra deli, cómigrauáo i mirabile fró
datura. Et alla dextra & finiftra pte femi pede itrauáo cũ elegáte politura
nel phrygio. Leq̃le fróde, q̃fi di tutto expffo fe uedeuano, & il fundo cioe
il plano fodo fubfidéte della corpulétia era dl hyacitho. In tutto da q̃fte
infrondate caude, era la corpulente circunferentia occupata, o uero cin
giente fafcicula dui pedi.

Refta a dire delliteruallo che exta uno pede & femi p lato. La corpu¿
létia del uafo del cócincto in giu, ftupéda opa iudicai & piu pfto diuina
Mirai el dicto uafo intecto per tutto duna exacta uite di fcalptura. Dellaquale gli ftupiti, o uero furculi pampinulati, cum uiticuli & anulati ca
preoli, di una uena accommodata ad lo excogitato di Topacio. Quale
non fe retrouarebbe nel infula Ophiade.

La foliatura di finiffimo fmaragdo, Gli racemi di Amethifto. O q̃to

l iii

allintuito præftauafi iucundiffimo,&allo intellecto gratiofamente con-
téplabile.Il fubiecto folido delq̃le feiũcta era q̃fta opatura & exacta,pluce
ua del hyacitho,piu terfo & rotõdato,q̃le al torno nõ fi farebbe cõducto.
Solaméte fotto alle foglie,era uno tenue relicto, che retiniua el foliaméto
cũ el fubiecto hyacitho,tutto puio & dal fubiecto feparato q̃fi policario.
Le finuate foglie.cũ tutti gli liniaméti accefforii fabre depolite,cũ temera
ria æmulatiõedella natura,nõ meno unq̃tulo fructi pápini & errãti fur-
culi.Ad q̃fta miráda factura nũ fe æq gli pocoli dil diuo Alchimedóte.
Ne ácora la copa di Alcone.Ilq̃le uafe era cópleto de minuto & fcõ cíere.
   Retorniamo allambiéte cinctura dl ptiofiffimo uafo,o uero phrygia
le fafcia.Nel uacuo tra le caude relicto,Vidi due hiftoriale digne di maxi
ma admiratióe í tale fcalptura.Nella facia dinãti di effo uafo mirai í cifu-
ra optimáméte lo altitonante Ioue.Ello nella dextra mano teniua una ta
gliéte fpatha aurea di uena di Chryfolithodi æthiopia lápadáte.Nelaltra
uno fulmíe corufcáte di uena rubinacea.Et egli cũ minãte afpecto de ue
na Gallatite coronato di fcintillante ftelle q̃le el fulmine. Sopra ftante de
uno facro altare Zaphirico.Nella diuina & treméda maieftate dlq̃le guar
dai uno feftiuáte choro de fette Nymphe cadide di íduméto, religiofamé
te ídicádo di cátare, eũ uenerabódo plaufo.Leq̃le pofcia fe trãfformauáo
in uerdigiáte arbore di fmaragdina pfpicuitate,cóferte di flofculi Cyanei
plucéti.Et al fúmo Numine fediuotaméte íclinauano . Non che tutte le
Nymphe fufferon tramutate i frõde,Ma la nouiffima eéndo tutta i arhu-
fculo cóuerfa,& gli pedi í radicule,& la uicina gli pedi exclufi, & la tertia,
dal cingere fupra.cũ lo exordio degli brachii & fubfequéte ciafcuna po-
fcia.Ma nella fúmitate del uirgineo capo ídicauáo el metamorphofi che
de tutte doueua fucceffiuamente fequire.

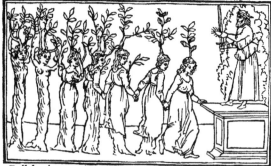

   Dallaltro lato anaglypho appareua uno feftiuo &iucundo Nume,cũ
fembiãte di una lubrica fanciulla,ícoronato di dui lungi & cóglobati fer
                                   pi luno

pi,lo uno biaco,&laltro negro,cú uiuace fpirule inodati. Staua effo uo
lupticaméte collocato fotto di una fœcúda uite.Sopra della quale per,
gulata,faliuano nel uolto ridibondi alcuni belliffimi fpiritelli nudi. Et
dindi gli péduli & grauidi racemi maturi extirpauáo, A lcúi accortamé
te ad q́fto diuo Numegli offeriuáo negli calathi.Et egli auidutofi placi,
daméte gli receueua.Alcuni nel uerdaceo folo iaceuáo refupini,al dol,
ce fomno puocati dal uuaceo fucco. Altri itétaméte faceuáo la opa del
muftuléto Autúno.Altri cú gli extéti Tympani ociofaméte fonáti cá,
tilauano.Lequale expreffione,fecundo la exigétia degli coloraméti,cu,
fi eráo naturalméte le uene al diffinito excogitato dellartifice,della pre,
tiofa petra opportunaméte accefforie,Et in q́fte imaguncule,q́túq̃; par,
uicule,Niente di meno,defecto alcuno, & nelle minime parte fe accufa
ua.Ma omni parte diftinctaméte pfecta cerneuafe.

Fora del pfcripto uafo,germinaua una fródofa uite doro cum gli ir,
riciati pampini, fœtofaméte ornata de Botriculi,cú grani punicei de in
dico Amethyfto,& la foliatura del fancto Silenite di Perfida uerdigian
te,Ad gli inoti Lunarii nó fubdito,Et a Cupidie placido.Præferuáte fo
fpite il gerulo,& ombricaua la Seiuga.

In ciafcúo águlo della plana,del triúphale carro,diffufaméte fpléde
fceua,collocato uno faberrimo cádelabro,fopra tre pediculi cornicula,
ti fúdato,di ramicofo coralio,pftabile adgli ruricoli. Fulmini.Typhói.
& repelléte le tépeftate,& al portitore benigno & Amuleto.Quale Simi
láte nó fue fotto el capo Gorgóeo da Perfeo retrouato,Ne tale nel Ery,
thromare,Ne lace nel Perfico,Ne tale el Drepáico.Dapofcia ad uno de,
gli q́li tutto el ftylo era de ceruleo & lufitáo ceraunioſi amicabile delle té
peftate,& di Diana amicale pcipuo,cú tépata corpulétia,& gracilaméto
de lógiufculi balufti & noduli.Cú obftétatióe fpectabile , di uermicula,
ria opatura adornati,de altitudine bipedale.Laltro pftauafe de finiffima

Dionyſia petra,cũ macule í nigritudine rubéte,el Numetrita

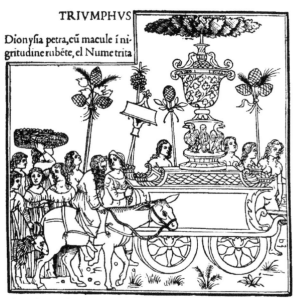

oléte. Il tertio deoptía Medea,i fuſco aureo colore diſſemíato,cũ el Ne-
ctareo ſapore.Lo ultío ð ptioſa Nebride,al Numedicata,Nel nigro exi
mio colore bianco & uiride immixtamente coeunte. Nella cóchula de
gli ꝗli,una Pyramidale flámula,di foco íextíguibile continua ardeua .

Per laꝗle luculétia le eximie opature & expſſi,p lo reflexo del flámicu
láte lũe,p li fulguráti lapilli ptioſiſſimi pſeuerátemte ſpectare nó ualeua.

Circa ðlꝗle diuino triũpho,cũ multa & ſoléne ſupſtitióe & maxía pó
pa & religióe Infinite Nymphe Mænade cũ li ſoluti & ſparſi capilli.Al
cũe nude cũ amiculi Nymphei dagli humeri deflui, & tale Nebride,
cioe ídute depelliceo uariato ð colore di damule,ſenza laltro ſexo,Cym
baliſtrie,& Tibiciarie,faceuáo le ſacre Orgie,cũ clamori uociferádo , &
thyaſi,ꝗle negli Trieterici,cũ thyrſi di fróde di cóiſere arbore, & cũ fron
de uitine íſtrophiate,ſopra el nudo cíéte & coróate ſaltatorie,pcuréte ſeꝗ
ua ímediate el triũpho ſiléo ſeniculo lo aſello eqtáte,Poſcia retro a ꝗſto
eqtáte ímediate uno Hirco horricome de ſacrifica pópa ornata feſtiua-
méte códuceuáo. Et una ð ꝗſto ſectaria,uno uiminaceo Váno geſtaua,
cũ deſordíato riſo,& furiali geſti,cũ ꝗſto ueterrimo & ſcó rito, ꝗſto ꝗrto
triũpho adoriaméte extolleuano,Et có uenerádo diſcorſo Euibache ad
alta uoce,cófuſaméte exclamádo gli Mimalloni.Satyri.Bacche.Lene.
Thyade.Naiade.Tityri.nymphe,celebrabondi ſequiuano.

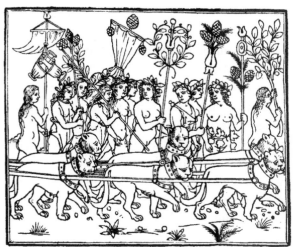

LA MVLTITVDINE DEGLI AMANTI GIOVENI, ET
DILLE DIVE AMOROSE PVELLE LA NYMPHA APOLI
PHILO FACVNDAMENTE DECHIARA, CHI FVRO‑
NO ET COMEDAGLI DII AMATE. ET GLI CHORI DE
GLI DIVI VATICANTANTI VIDE.

 LCVNO MAI DITANTO INDEFESSO E LO
quio aptamente se accommodarebbe, che gli diuini ar
chani disertando copioso & pienamente potesse euade
re & uscire. Et expressamente narrare, & cum quanto di
ua pompa, indesinenti Triumphi, perenne gloria, festi
ua lætitia, & fœlice tripudio, circa a queste quatro iuisi
tate seiuge de memorando spectamine cum parole sufficientemente ex‑
primere ualesse. Oltra gli inclyti adolescentuli & stipante agmine di inu‑
mere & periucunde Nymphe, piu che la tenerecia degli anni sui elle pru‑
dente & graue & astutule cum gli acceptissimi amanti de pubescente
& depile gene. Ad alcuni la primula lanugine splendescéte le male in‑
serpiua delitiose alacremente festigiauano. Molte hauendo le farole sue
accense & ardente. Alcune uidi Pastophore. . Altre cum drite haste
adornate de prische spolie. Et tali di uarii Trophæi optimaméte ordinate

VI. THE BEGINNING OF THE ALDINE PRESS

THE FIRST DATED BOOK PUBLISHED BY ALDUS was issued in 1495. It was the Greek Grammar of Constantine Lascaris, first printed in Milan in 1476, but scarce by the time Aldus reprinted it. It would seem from the imprint of the Lascaris *(Literis ac impensis Aldi Manutii Romani)* and from the subsequent Theocritus *(Caracteribus ac studio A.M.R.)* that for those two publications, at least, Aldus might not have had his own shop but was the owner of the type used to set the books and had given them his editorial attention. These two books might well have issued from Andrea Torresani's press at San Paternian.

The first volume of Aldus' grand project to reprint Aristotle in a five-volume folio set appeared in 1495. It carries not only a dedication to Alberto Pio indicating that Aldus' former pupil contributed financially to the great enterprise, but also the message of Aldus' life work in an editorial program which is, for him, a moral imperative and for his contemporaries a crowning achievement in the recovery of the classics and the growth of learning in the West. Noting the wars and conflicts that rend Italy, he hopes to counterbalance that ferocity by diffusing instead the wealth of humanity in the guise of poetry, beauty, and wisdom.

In 1496, with the volume of Gaza, the imprint changes, as if Aldus were now at last truly in possession of a printing shop. The books that he issues now bear the designation *in aedibus Aldi,* or *in domo Aldi,* or simply *apud Aldum,* "at Aldo's." This first printing location for the Aldine press was in Calle del Pistor, facing the church at Campo Sant'Agostin.

Occasionally Aldus, in his prefaces, will deviate from his scholarly commentary and take note of external events.[34] In the preface to his first book printed in Greek, the *Hero and Leander* of 1494, he takes note of "the great wars that infest Italy, the wrath of God against our sins, that will soon move all the world." It is a year of defeat as well as of personal sorrow for Aldus. On the same day that Charles VIII of France entered Florence and Lorenzo de' Medici's magnificent library was sacked and scattered, Giovanni Pico della Mirandola died at the age of thirty-one, followed only

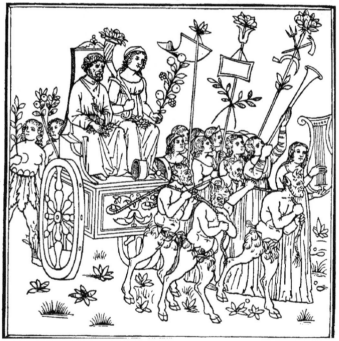

INTEGERRIMAM CORPOR. VALITVDINEM ET STABILE
ROBVR CASTASQUE MENSAR. DELITIAS ET BEATAM
ANIMI SECVRITATEM CVLTORIB. M. OFFERO.

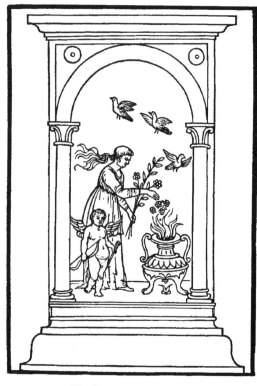

FLORIDO VERI. S.

two months later by the sudden death of Poliziano at forty.

The echo of war and tumult and national convulsion that is present in Aldus' first preface will repeat itself during the twenty years of his publishing career; and one of the few contemporary writings he will publish is the *De bello Carolino* on Charles VIII's Italian invasion. In 1498 the plague reached Venice, and Aldus was stricken. Fellow-humanist Marsilio Ficino, who was to be curator of an Aldine edition of Synesius, wrote to Aldus in 1498 that he, too, was taken ill:

*

"Three furies torment our already wretched Florence, the plague, hunger, and revolt." It is also the year that Savonarola was burned at the stake. Thinking himself on his death-bed, Aldus vowed to dedicate his life to God as a religious if he survived. With his recovery, however, and his resumption of his editorial program, the idea of entering the religious life faltered, and he invoked Pope Alexander VI to dissolve his vow, which was granted through the patriarch of Venice.

His enthusiasm as publisher again at full peak, in 1498 Aldus saw the last volume of the Aristotle through the press. It was to be followed by the whole of Aristophanes with the exception of *Lysistrata,* of which Aldus possessed only half the text. Aldus' friends and collaborators call him affectionately "il papà dei libri."[35] The publication of the Greek Aristotle occupied Aldus from 1495 to 1498.

*

* * *

*

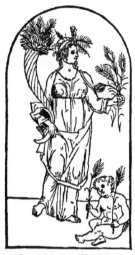

FLAVAE MESSI .S.

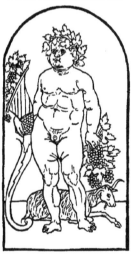

MVSTVLENTO
AVTVMNO .S.

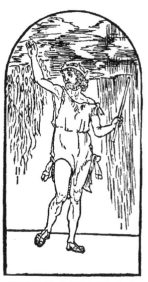

HYEMI AEOLIAE .S.

It is an *editio princeps,* the first time the works of Aristotle have appeared together, some available for the first time since antiquity, and lacking only the *Rhetoric* and *Poetics,* which were then unobtainable, but which would be added later. It is a noble endeavor and Aldus' title to glory. The Greek edition of Aristotle has been called the greatest scholarly and printing achievement of the fifteenth century. Aldus' merits as a scholar-publisher are achieved, and to these he will add typographical ones.

PRINTING had been born with the angular Gothic letters of the North still used in manuscripts, even though Italian humanism tempered that angular face into something tending towards the ancient Roman hand. Gothic was bushy, gross, and full, and it carried over into printing the manuscript habit of frequent abbreviations. Another style of the old codices, which was at first carried over into printing, was the format of two columns per page. With Jenson's creation of a beautiful clear roman face with fine capitals, the look of the Renaissance book comes into being.

*

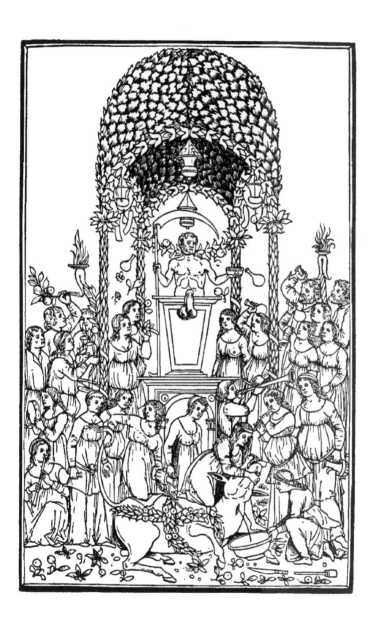

Aldus took up Jenson's clean-lined roman, confirming by his imposing editorial activity the use of the new characters. Aldus used roman type in his first Latin publication, Pietro Bembo's *De Aetna* of 1495, but continued throughout his career to modify and improve the face.

From his initial use of Greek in the early works, through the small, almost ligatureless characters of the 1502 Sophocles, Aldus constantly experimented and invented, and at least six different typefaces in Greek can be distinguished in that period. Aldus' humanist interest in manuscripts is evident in his formation of a typeface that will look like a natural hand. Even though attempts to duplicate calligraphic connections and ligatures will be given up by other printers in the interest of greater legibility, Aldus' type continues to have a certain cursive slant that imparts a particular elegance to it. Aldus also uses ornamental capitals and borders so that the pleasing impression is conveyed that manuscript art is not totally abandoned to mechanical form.

Aldus himself oversaw the achievement of the "divine proportion" of the page, as well as the essential architectural element of the type. In that peak of Renaissance aesthetics and concern with beauty and divine proportion, the printing of the classics in book format could hardly ignore classical canons of form. Aldus was therefore concerned with the just distribution of type composition over the page, sufficient margins, and well-set lines.

Aldus also gave great care to providing type that was aesthetically pleasing by seeking out the best goldsmiths or metal-workers to incise punches and matrixes for type-casting. He had them imitate the hand in manuscripts as the best models. His partiality to cursive style led him to "think out" a new

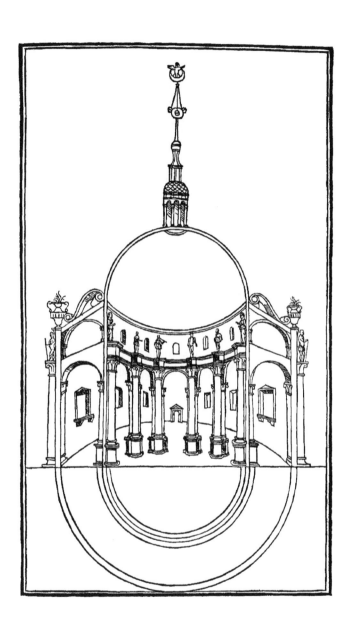

typeface, to be called "italic," which he previewed with five words that appeared on the pages of an open book held by St. Catherine of Siena in a woodcut illustration to her letters, *Epistole devotissime,* published in 1500.

* *
*

IT IS DEBATABLE whether Aldus inaugurated italic strictly in his zeal to produce a type that more nearly imitated handwrit‚ ing or whether he had also conceived that he could reduce the cost of producing printed books by reducing the page size of his books through the use of the slanted letter. He commissioned the cutting of an italic type and petitioned the Senate for protection of the characters. The new typeface he refers to as "a Latin chancery and cursive letter of surpassing beauty which seems as written by the very hand." Aldus based it upon the hand commonly used for correspondence and records in the papal chancery. In 1431 the Vatican chancery had adopted a beautiful and clear formal style of handwriting that became known as the chancery hand, and it was this model that Aldus referred to. When it appeared, others came to call the new typeface *Aldino,* thus making the connec‚ tion to Aldus. It is a fine running letter, light and slanted, neatly proportioned in legible smallness to fit the lines of the new small book. Italic was more compressed than roman face and could fit more words to a line. It had also the aesthetic advantage for Aldus of more closely resembling handwriting – the cursive hand, or *corsiva* – which to him, in all his printing career, was his first aim. The first complete book in italic was essentially the first modern book, the octavo, hand‚sized Virgil of 1501. Aldus inserted on the title-page verso of this book a three-line verse in Latin which reads:

> Lo! Aldus, who gave letters to the Greeks, now
> gives them, engraved by the Daedalian hands
> of Francesco da Bologna, to the Latins.

Aldus had his italic letter cut by Francesco Griffo, then identified merely as Francesco da Bologna, and in the tribute paid to his skill, Aldus used the term "Daedalian" to mean that Francesco's consummate artistry rivaled that of the fabled artisan Daedalus. Despite the acknowledgment, it must have seemed too little to the type-cutter. Francesco Griffo had a falling out with Aldus, perhaps feel-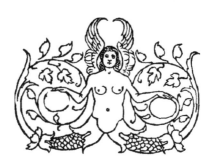ing deprived of his own glory and earnings. He is known to have made duplicate punches of the italic letter for the printer Girolamo Soncino of Fano, who, in the preface to a 1503 italic edition of Petrarch, castigates Aldus for maltreating Francesco and for having secured a mo-nopoly on the typeface in Venetian and papal territories. Aldus had indeed petitioned the Venetian Senate for a ten-year privilege for the exclusive use of italic to prevent its usurpation in Venetian territory. The notice of his privilege was published in the edition of Horace, which followed Virgil by a month.

* *
*

THE INCUNABULA, the first products of the printing press, were large folio volumes. Aldus himself was printing folio or quarto-size editions at the start of his publishing career. The year 1501 also saw the publication of two beautiful folio volumes of treatises on arithmetic, music, geometry, astrology

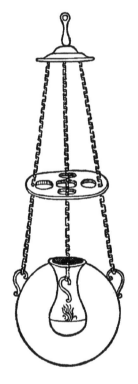

etc. by Giorgio Valla. They have been dismissed as "two splendid volumes, with absolutely nothing interesting in them."[36] On the contrary, there is a great deal of interest to be garnered from the fact that the text is set throughout in roman face but the illustrative notes used with figures and diagrams are in italic, thus prenoting the modern use of italic – i.e., as emphasis or to set it off from the text.

The real revolution, the moment of true divulgation of the printed word that impelled Western society on its linear way, came when Aldus brought out his edition of Virgil's *Georgics* in the elegant, octavo format that was to become the staple of the Aldine press and Aldus' trademark. His preface to the 1514 edition of Virgil is dedicated to Pietro Bembo and recalls that his small book format is derived from seeing manuscript copies of certain classics in small size as with books of hours or other works of private devotion in the library of Bembo's father. Aldus intended a "handy" book, in the shape of a manual or handbook, and in his

June 22, 1503 catalog he described his octavo editions as *libri portatiles*.[37] Prices for unbound books in Latin are thirty soldi, 1½ lire; those in Greek are twice the price. The five-volume folio Aristotle, his most expensive item, was just under thirteen gold ducats, the equivalent of 1,612 soldi, and still unaffordable for a schoolmaster who made fifty ducats a year or a government secretary earning about eighty.[38]

Aldus had produced a book that could be set in a new, compact type, saving white space. It was small enough to put in a pocket to take on a journey or to read easily without having to have it propped up by a great wooden lectern. It was inexpensive enough for students and scholars who wandered between Europe's great universities. It was the precise and elegant result of a scrupulous and thorough collation of manuscript sources, producing the most authoritative, critical text possible.

Aldus' pocket-sized Virgil was the gesture of a true humanist scholar as well as of an astute publisher – Virgil had been Dante's guide and the epitome of all that was revered in classical learning, the seer and prophet, the true link from the ancient world through the medieval and into the beginning of the modern era.

With the publication of this renowned – and now very rare – edition of the *Georgics* was presented the concept of the small book, the modern book. As with anything new, the octavo book was at first sniffed at. Yet its practicality caught on. Following Virgil's *Georgics,* every month thereafter, a new octavo edition of the classics issued from Aldus' press – a book-of-the-month, which could not be denigrated. Each book with the dolphin and anchor imprint represented the combination of steadiness and precipitous zeal that marked

Aldus' enterprise. In 1501, with his publication of an octavo Petrarch in italic, the first volume in vernacular Italian issued from the Aldine press.

Oddly, however, Aldus had not provided italic capitals for his new typeface and used roman capitals with his lower case italic. In his last will and testament, after provisions for his burial and masses for his soul, there is a moving last statement pertaining to unfinished business: "In addition, since there is still to be refined that cursive character that we call chancery, I appeal to my father-in-law Andrea that he have it re-worked and perfected by Giulio Campagnola who should execute the capitals that have to accompany the chancellery letters."

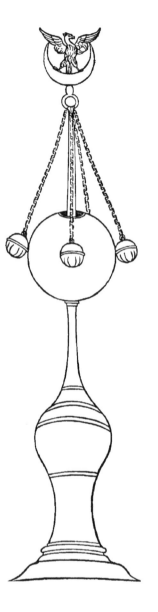

*

WHEN Aldus speaks of his father-in-law he refers to Andrea Torresani, the printer whom he had long known, and whose daughter, Maria, Aldus married in 1505 when she was twenty and he fifty-five.

The following year, 1506, Aldus and Andrea went into partnership and pooled their assets (Aldus having one part to Andrea's four) to form one printing establishment at San Paternian. Books from this press are identified in colophons as issuing *in aedibus Aldi et Andreae soceri,* which indicates a joint domicile at the print shop. And so it was.

Aldus, who had led such a monkish and austere life for so long, may have been induced to marriage by the prospect of the dowry of ducats that Maria Torresani brought him, and it may have also been a practical consideration contingent to Aldus' partnership with her father Andrea, and his moving into Andrea's home. After their association, Aldus left Calle del Pistor and crossed the Grand Canal to the San Paternian *rione* where Andrea had his shop and home. There is a letter of 1505 from Alberto Pio to Aldus, in which Alberto regrets he could not make the wedding, but inviting the newlyweds to Carpi as soon as Aldus recovers from the illness that took him shortly after his marriage. In a teasing allusion made possible because of the intimacy between the two, Alberto adds that he's sure it's passing and doubts not but that the indisposition probably came from "having abstained so long a time from such a feast as to have overdone yourself in satiating desire once and for all."

Instead of honeymooning, Aldus plunged into his work. Among the new issues from his press were the *Fables* of Aesop; Pietro Bembo's dialogs on courtly love in the vernacular tongue, *Gli Asolani;* the works of the Neapolitan humanist Giovanni Pontano; and Demosthenes. In this latter work Aldus alludes to what is presently happening politically in Italy, hoping that the example of the great Greek orator, defender of his country against the foreign invader, will help invigorate Italian hearts and

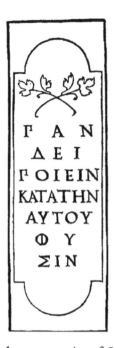

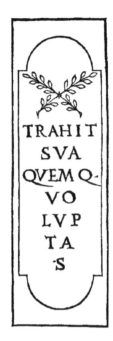

consolidate their civil virtues.

For Italy, once again, was in crisis; a new storm was gathering on the horizon instigated by France, the German Empire, and the pope and aimed directly at Venice.

It is just at this precarious moment, in the summer of 1506, that Aldus undertook a trip to search out a particular manuscript of Virgil. Given his absence from Venice, he proceeded to make out the first of his wills, indicating that he has property at Carpi and Ferrara in addition to his printing establishment at Calle del Pistor. At the same time, he reinforced the partnership with his father-in-law. Aldus' journey seems to have a lasted a year during which his first-born son, Manuzio, was born. He returned to Venice with renewed vigor and material for further editions.

* *
*

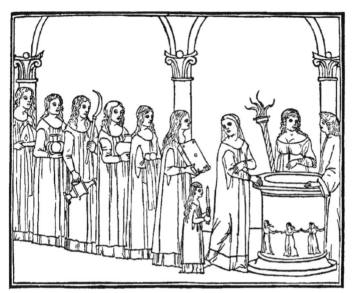

ALDUS' NAME is also connected with a certain style of book binding that was new and came from the East whence it was then diffused in Venice by the book industry there. Binding had become an artistic activity in Venice, and the first notices to the binder, which Aldus included in the second volume of his Aristotle (1497), are given in Greek. In fact, the new technical system used is called "binding in the Greek style" and is carried out by specialized workers who are usually Greek. It requires a folding of sheets at their spine in order to contain the threads on which the book is bound in its cover. Moroccan leather is used, most often in a pale olive color, and gold impressions of simple, stylized flowers or entwined geometrical embellishments are added. The first bound books retained the bronze closures of the old manuscript style, then they were completely eliminated.

PIERRE DE NOLHAC, a French authority on Aldus, pointed out the long delay the progress of intellectual culture would have undergone if Aldus had not gone into publishing determined not only to preserve the Hellenic patrimony but to diffuse it. Aldus asked all over Europe for manuscripts; and they came from every part, including Poland and Hungary. The Venetian Alvise Mocenigo brought him the Paris Codex of Pliny's letters; from the library in Vienna of the Holy Roman Emperor came twenty-four codices; the volume of Astronomy of 1499 included the *Procli diadochi sphaera,* which the English humanist Thomas Linacre sent Aldus. His aim was to find even better texts of what was already extant so that he could emend and print the best version that would become, if not a defini-tive text – since he was always open to re-examination based on superior versions – at least a decent standard for his time. Some manuscripts were given to him, others sold, and sometimes, according to Erasmus, the manuscripts were accompanied by honoraria so that printing costs were covered.

$$* \quad *$$
$$*$$

ALDUS' world-famous trademark, the emblem of the an-chor
and the dolphin, is perhaps the most celebrated of all
printers' marks, and in its graceful design, classical
reference, and the meaning of the *festina lente*
motto, which derives from it – that is,
Hasten Slowly – it is eminently
suited to the scholar-printer
who would adopt it.[39]

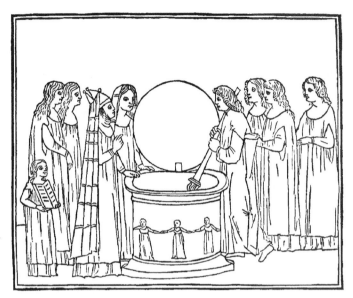

Aldus had already used the Greek form of the motto in his preface to the collected works of Angelo Poliziano published in July 1498. In his dedicatory letter to Marin Sanudo, Aldus says he has kept the adage in mind in preparing the edition. The Latin version first appeared in an October 14, 1499 letter to Prince Alberto of Carpi, where Aldus writes: "I am my own best witness that the Dolphin and Anchor are my constant companions; for I have accomplished much by delay and continue to do so."

Aldus first used this emblem in the vertical, as the emblem of the Aldine press in the 1502 edition of *Poetae christiani veteres*. It is found depicted horizontally in the *Hypnerotomachia Poliphili* of 1499 as one of its classically inspired illustrations. In his *Adages*, Erasmus gives an account of the emblem, from its classical allusion in Suetonius, as a favorite of the Emperor

Augustus. Erasmus goes on to say that at the time he was a guest of Aldus in Venice, he was shown an ancient silver coin of Titus' reign with that device engraved on it, which had been given to Aldus by Pietro Bembo some years earlier, around 1490. One side of the coin depicted Titus with the motto, the other showed the anchor (caution) with the dolphin (speed) twisted around it as visible interpretation of the saying. And if it is considered that it took Aldus until his forty-third year to prepare himself for his publishing career, the motto is indeed apt.

"Actually," Erasmus concludes, "I don't think this symbol was more famous at that time when it was shown on an imperial coin and passed from hand to hand of merchants, than now when together with the volumes of that ancient era it is diffused to all nations...."[40]

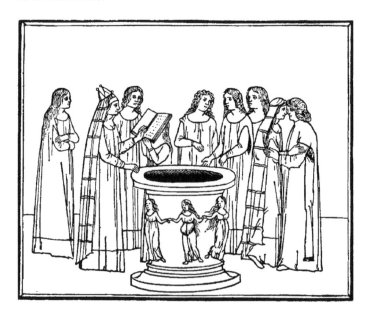

VII. THE *HYPNERTOMACHIA POLIPHILI*

GIVEN ALDUS' NATURAL PROCLIVITY TOWARDS
seriousness and an austere morality, plus his deathbed pledge to
dedicate himself in full to the religious life if he is spared, it is
rather surprising that his great endeavor following his recovery
was the printing in 1499, at the close of the age of incunabula,
of that somewhat scurrilous and certainly paganized book of
the pursuit of love, the *Hypnerotomachia Poliphili,* the most
glorious book of the Renaissance, profusely illustrated and beautifully ornamented, which to this day remains a mystery, a text of
symbols and bizarre jargon in various languages and dialects.
Is the *Polifilo* a monstrous work, the slide of humanism into
its dotage, or the supreme philosophical poem of the fifteenth
century? It carries the spirit of humanism in which the senses
were substituted for conscience, but coming out thirty-two years
after it was written, it was already an echo of a past age when
humanistic passions were more fully engaged.

It is, nevertheless, a marvel of graphic beauty and variegated
composition, the most beautiful of all books containing
wood-cut illustrations, and the undoubted masterpiece of the school of Venetian wood-engraving.
It has been celebrated through
the centuries.

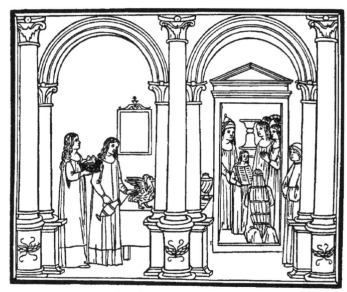

THE WORK is referred to variously as the *Hypnerotomachia,*
the *Poliphilus,* or in more recent usage, as in Martin Lowry, as
the *Polifilo* for its hero. It speaks for its age in being written in
1467 by a Dominican friar, Fra Francesco Colonna, at a time
when the passion for all things Greek and Roman, roused by
the revival of learning, was at its peak. The work was unsigned,
but the author reveals his name in an acrostic composed of
initial letters at the beginning of each chapter, and there is also
reference to him in a dedicatory poem by Matteo Visconti of
Brescia.[41] Francesco Colonna, of Treviso, was a friar since 1455
and lived from 1471 in the convent of SS. Giovanni e Paolo
(San Zanipolo) in Venice. He was sixty-six years old when his
work was published, and he died 1527.

The author who desired to remain anonymous – for obvious
reasons, given his religious status – still coyly reveals himself

through the device of having the initials beginning each chapter spell out: *Poliam Frater Franciscus Columna peramavit* (Friar Francesco Colonna desperately loved Polia). The theme is a lover's journey in quest of his sought-for but ever unobtainable mistress: the elusive Polia represents partly a woman loved and forfeited in real life, partly an abstract and spiritual ideal that can never be gained and possessed in mortal form.

The work seems clearly autobiographical. Polia's final pun to Polifilo is, "Thou art the solid column and culmination of my life." In Italian, column is *colonna* – again the signature of Fra Colonna who wanted both anonymity and to be known through the clues that he left in abundance. The whole is a perfect statement of the strange divided life, culture, and personality of the monk Francesco Colonna, who lived to the venerable age of 94, his life filled with episodes of bravado and adventure, and who makes an appearance in Charles Reade's epic novel of the Renaissance, *The Cloister and the Hearth,* as a kind of rogue-monk, a master of versatility, a zealot in art, a sceptic in religion, and an impassioned defender of paganism.[42]

The name Polifilo is as cryptic as the rest of the title. It
has usually been taken to mean "the lover of Polia"
and thought to be based on a real Italian woman,
possibly Lucrezia Lelli, supposedly the niece of
Fra Colonna's bishop, and analogous to
Dante's having used the image
of Beatrice in the
Divine Comedy.

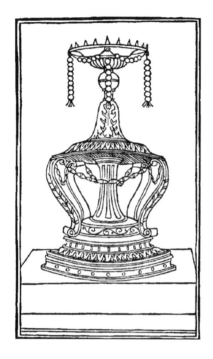

Polia, it is revealed in the text, is a girl of Treviso, who reached "the flower of her life" – possibly somewhere between her twelfth and sixteenth year – in 1462 but was already dead from plague in 1467 when Colonna finished his work. In the narrative Polifilo wakes from his dream of Polia in Treviso on the first of May, the traditional day of sweethearts. In 1710, De la Monnoye first voiced the thesis that Polia is not simply based on a real woman but is an allegory of antiquity, since the Greek term *polia* means "old age" or "antiquity." Therefore Polifilo could be construed as the lover of antiquity as personified through a female personage.[43]

Intriguing is the "notorious ease with which the Renaissance transferred a Christian figure of speech to a pagan subject, or gave pagan features to a Christian theme…[yet] hybridization works both ways…and Renaissance art produced many images of Venus which resemble a Madonna or a Magdalen. An extreme instance is the *Hypnerotomachia*, in which Venus is pictured as a *mater dolorosa*, nourishing her infant son with tears…."[44]

Hypnerotomachia is a word coined from three Greek elements meaning dream, love, strife; the exceedingly rare English translation of 1592 is titled *The Strife of Love in a Dream.* Hence the complete title of the work could be rendered as "Polia's Lover's Strife of Love in a Dream," with the further subtitle, *ubi humana omnia non nisi somnium esse docet,* wherein everything here narrated in human guise is nothing but a dream – a precursor of Shakespeare's lines a century later from *The Tempest:* "We are such stuff /As dreams are made on, and our little life / Is rounded with a sleep."

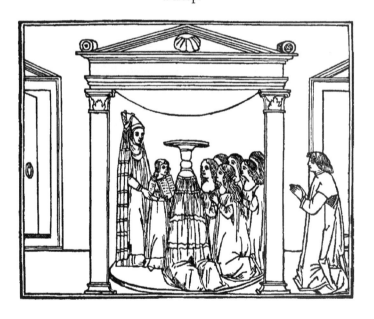

THERE IS A STORY in the curious work: Polifilo, in love with Polia, dreams at length of many antiquities; he is in a forest from which he emerges with great difficulty to come upon a grandiose building guarded by a terrifying dragon. Polifilo flees until he comes upon five nymphs in whose company he arrives at a splendid palace; here he finds Polia who takes him to the temple of Queen Eleutherylida and later to watch pageants depicting various myths of Jove, Bacchus, Vertumnus, Pomona, and Priapus; they visit temples and sacred woods, take part in dances and mysterious ceremonies, read ancient epigraphs, and contemplate architectural wonders, statues, ruins and inscriptions, finally participating in rites in honor of Venus and Cupid. Then they proceed with Cupid in a boat rowed by six nymphs to Cytheria, visit the tomb of Adonis and hear an account of the honors paid to him.

Within the main story Polia relates her own sad tale mentioning the origin of the Lellis in Treviso.[45] While smitten with the plague Polia had vowed herself to Diana, and thus to a chaste life if spared. But when Polifilo declares his love for her, she so pities him and is so fearful of Eros' vengeance on obstinate maidens that she yields to him. Driven from the temple for their act, they appeal to Venus who unites them in marriage. Then Polia disappears. With this the dream ends, and Polifilo wakes to find himself in Treviso on Friday, the first of May 1467.

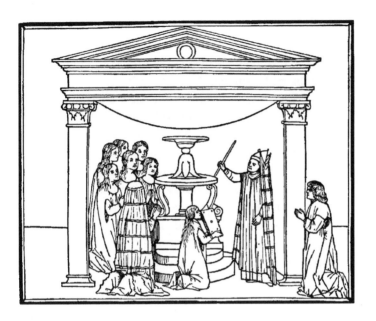

THE NARRATIVE is divided into two parts, of which the second is a shorter and simpler account of Polifilo's love, Polia's long resistance, pity's victory and Polifilo's awakening from his dream. Part Two seems to have been written before Part One – the prolix account of Polifilo's dream wanderings and the pretext for long, minute digressions into analytical descriptions of architecture, rituals, and ancient uses. It seems to attach to the simple story line a kind of humanist encyclopedia. Antiquity is the main focus; and the language is a mix of Italian, Venetian dialect, Latin, Greek, some Hebrew, Chaldean and Arabian and the author's own fantasy, all meant to convey a sense of the archaic, which is emphasized by an inversion of phrases and deliberate mystification. Appropriately enough, this mix of languages as a stylistic device was termed *"pedantesca."* It will prenote Joyce's portmanteau jargon of mixed meanings and languages in *Finnegan's Wake,* "a jetsam litterage of convolvuli of times lost or strayed, of lands derelict and of tongues laggin too."[46]

Thus it is not only the book's title that is abstruse; the work remained for a long while dense with unrecognizable symbols and an often indecipherable prose. After the original Aldine edition of 1499, and a succeeding one in 1545, the center of studies and speculation on the mystery of the *Polifilo* centered in France.[47] A French translation of 1546 was reissued in 1554 and 1561. François Béroalde de Verville's Paris edition of 1600 is a free adaptation of the text with, in addition, his essay on the alchemical lore contained in the work.

Béroalde's title reveals his thesis that there are veiled mysteries in the *Polifilo* that he has set out to decipher: *Le tableau des riches inventions couvertes du voile des feintes amoureuses, qui sont representées dans le SONGE DE POLPHILE desvoilées des ombres du songe e subtilmente exposées.*

* *
*

ALTHOUGH the five-volume Aristotle was to remain Aldus' scholarly masterwork, typographically speaking it was to be surpassed by the *Polifilo.* As a literary work it is called a *bizzarria* by Benedetto Croce, full of strange symbolism and linguistic improvisations; yet in its physical properties as a book it is one of the most beautiful examples ever to issue from a press. The work is illustrated by over two hundred woodcuts, of which 171 are drawings illustrating the text, including eleven full-page illustrations and thirty-nine floral capitals. The woodcuts are unsigned, although a lower-case letter "b" appears in the third illustration depicting Polifilo asleep on the ground under a tree. The woodcuts are superb, although in most extant copies of the work it seems that the engravings of some of the more phallic illustrations have been tampered with, possibly in Aldus' shop, or omitted outright.[48] An exemplar of the *Polifilo* in the Vatican Library shows examples of censorship in several

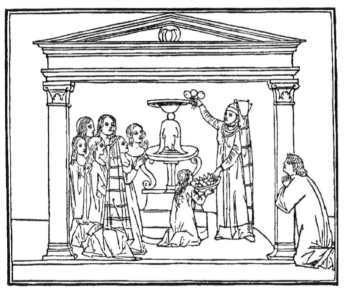

illustrations.[49] Because of this, a perfect specimen of the original *Polifilo* is seldom seen. However, the Antenore edition from Padua in 1964, under the typographical supervision of famed Verona printer, Giovanni Mardersteig, does carry unexpurgated illustrations. This important critical and annotated edition provides a second volume of commentary to the text.[50]

It has to be wondered what the rigorous-minded and abstemious Aldus thought of Colonna's work, aside from the printing challenge it presented. The whole book has been called "an extraordinary exhibit of what an ingenious printer can accomplish within the limitations of metal type."[51] It represents perfectly the spirit of Italian culture at the end of the fifteenth century when neoclassicism had slipped over into a kind of hypersophistication.

The publication was commissioned by and published at the expense of Leonardo Crasso, a well-to-do lawyer of Verona in whose name it must have been copyrighted. A document of 1508 shows him petitioning the Venetian Senate for a ten-year extension of his copyright on the ground that from the time that he took out the previous one, the decade was so full of civic tumult and war disrupting trade, that much of the edition of the *Hypnerotomachia Poliphili* remained unsold. The work is dedicated to Guidobaldo, duke of Urbino, whose name certainly lent respectability to the unusual subject matter.

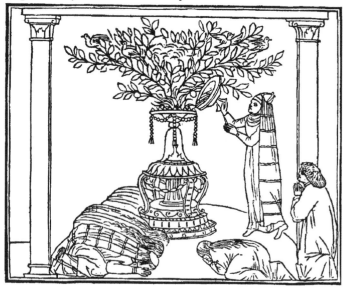

IT IS SOMETIMES said that Aldus minimized his part in the publication of the *Polifilo* because his name is not conspicuous but appears only on the errata page, in a small, modest print but with a vaunting last word: "Venetiis Mense decembri MID in aedibus Aldi Manutii, accuratissime." From Aldus' point of view, however, the importance of the *Polifilo* is in the first appearance there of the Aldine roman typeface in its finished form. The basic design had already been used in another version for other works, but not until the *Polifilo* was printed had a body size suitable for the typeface and a harmony between capitals and lower case been fully achieved. This roman letter became the ancestor of all the modern "oldface" types, which descend from it through Garamond, Van Dyk, and Caslon.

The book itself was such a creation of beauty that it does not seem credible that Aldus would have wanted to minimize his own part in its production from his press. The folio volume of 234 leaves displays a harmony of illustration and text that is amazing for its day and established it among the master works of printing of all ages. Whatever Aldus may have thought of the subject matter, it is perhaps not accidental that he followed the paganish *Polifilo* with the publication in 1500 of the *Epistole* of St. Catherine at his own full expense.

*

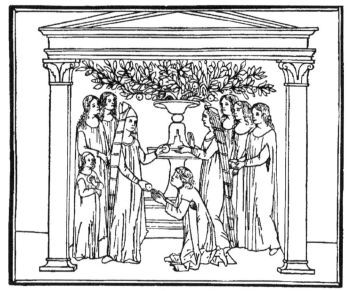

THE *POLIFILO* remains one of the most celebrated, enigmatic, and un-read books that exist. Not long after the work came out, Castiglione referred to it sarcastically in *The Courtier* when he mentioned lovers who think it necessary to converse in the manner of *Polifilo*, thus making "an hour of such conversation seem like a thousand years."

Beyond the enduring typographical and bibliographical interest in this most precious of the incunabula, interest in our time has been revived in the *Polifilo* as a vehicle for the cultural thought of the late fifteenth century. Perhaps it is only in our time, with the intense interest in the psyche, in the unconscious and occult, in symbols and the kind of riddles that make *Finnegan's Wake* what it is, that we can properly appreciate and begin to unravel this strange fifteenth-century story of the pursuit of love told in allegory.

Linda Fierz-David, a friend and associate of Carl Jung, has done a masterly job in relating and interpreting the dream symbology to alchemy. Jung himself, whose imagination was greatly stirred by the occult and the hidden meaning in symbols, first saw a copy of the *Polifilo* in 1925 in Béroalde's French translation. Crasso, in his dedication, says that the book contains things not to be divulged to the ordinary populace, for they deal with matters drawn from the very heart of philosophy and the Muses. Thus, the impenetrable thicket of language is deliberately willed in order to keep hidden what it was not opportune to disclose. It contains erotica, a battle of the two cultures of Christianity and neo-paganism, and a philosophical Venus as the mother of all things. Perhaps, it has been speculated, the doctrine to be kept from the masses is the theory that nature is good, and each must do according to his or her nature.

Polia, who speaks for the sensate spirit of the Renaissance, frees Polifilo from his introverted obsession with alchemy and medieval restrictions. He is led back into classical culture, reconnected (via Polia) to ancient humanism, its psychological depths and erotic wisdom. Fierz-David interprets the narrative as a guidebook to and by the anima. She saw the work as expounding the plight of the Christian experiencing mysterious initiation into a new secular age. Since the Renaissance, she observes, the development of the secular personality has become common property, no longer a mystery.[52]

The whole idea of dreams being uncovered from the shadows of their inventive symbology is one that must have appealed strongly to Jung. It can be shown that Jung's studies in alchemy did not precede his acquaintanceship with Béroalde's alchemic interpretation of the *Polifilo,* so that it could have been Colonna's work that led Jung into those very fields of research. It was the illustration of the lamp represent, ing the alchemical credo of Mercury being at the center of all things that gave Béroalde de Verville his original insight into the *Polifilo* as an alchemical text.

Fierz,David thoroughly explores the three traditions on which the *Polifilo* is based and whose threads interweave in the

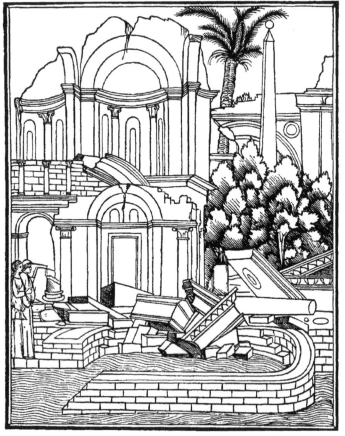

narrative—the humanist strand, the alchemical strand, and finally that of courtly love. She sees the crux of Polifilo's dilemma as his blindly seeking in the illusion of an actual woman and in the convention of courtly love the complement to himself that is already by his side — that is, the nymph who represents the anima and, thus, the reconciliation of opposites.

The narrative amply discloses the humanist and courtly love themes in the comparison of the *Strife of Love in a Dream* to *The Divine Comedy* in its opening pages. Polifilo is seen lost in a wood, confronted by different monstrous animals, while searching for his idealized love; the allusions to alchemy are disclosed in the illustrations and the deliberate arcaneness of a language made from so many different elements. Béroalde thought of the allegory as a manual of alchemy; the Jungians find in its quaternity the formula for individuation that leads to self-knowledge, with Fierz-David paralleling the ending to Faust; and finally, it has also been thought to be the application of Leon Battista Alberti's architectural theories from his treatise *De re aedificatoria.*

*

THAT IT IS a work of great richness beyond the always acknowledged treasures of its wood-cut illustrations is gradually coming to light. It was always acclaimed for its typographical perfection and has presented a constant challenge to art historians in identifying the Master of the Wood-Cuts, who, aside from the cryptic "b," was never identified in the text or the dedications. They have been variously attributed to Giovanni or Gentile Bellini; Andrea Mantegna; Carpaccio; to Radolt's partner, Bernard Pictor; to Benozzo Gozzoli; Cima da Conigliano; or, newly favored, Benedetto Bordone.[53]

GEORGE PAINTER CUTS THROUGH ALL THE
HYPOTHESES WITH HIS OWN THEORY THAT THE

aster of the Wood-Cuts was probably trained by Mantegna at Mantua and then worked for Giovanni Bellini in Venice, for it is the influence of these two great artists that is most strongly felt in the wood-cut illustrations. Painter further supposes that the master probably based his wood-cuts on Francesco Colonna's own drawings in his manuscript and that the only reason that he remains unknown as an artist in his own right is that he may have died young after having only produced one work, but that a masterpiece, the *Polifilo*.

Edgar Wind points out that "the woodcuts of the *Hypnerotomachia* alone show more than eighty variations of *festina lente,* each one of them giving a new twist to the theme. Some of the designs are frankly comical, like the image of elephants turning into ants, and of ants into elephants.... Still others are puzzles for the eye: there is the half-seated, half-rising figure of a girl who has placed one foot firmly on the ground while lifting the other high into the air. On the side of the stationary foot she holds a pair of wings, on the side of the lifted foot a tortoise.... Through such ciphers, which entertain while they instruct, the hero of the *Hypnerotomachia* is cautiously and alluringly guided towards the more hidden arcana, learning on his way to combine prudence with daring. The plan of the novel, so often quoted and so little read, is to 'initiate' the soul into its own secret destiny – the final union of Love and Death...."[54]

Though the work may newly interest us on psychological or literary levels, the *Polifilo* owes its survival, in fact, to its graphic beauty, its design and typographical composition.

tribune diſpoſite,p che ancora reliɕe erano alcune parte ſemiitegre,oue
ro ſemirute & fragmenti magni di pyle,cũ ſinuate trabe,& corni di teſtu-
dinato,& di procerecolũnedi uariata ſpecie,alcune numidice & alcune
hymettie & laconice tra le ſopranominate & altre ſorte uenuſtiſſime pure
& expedite di liniamento.Per la diſpoſitionedillequaletribune cuſi apta
mente iudicai,che in quelle locati fuſſeron gli ſepulchri.

 In queſto loco ananti tute coſe,alla parte poſtica di eſſo archæo tempio mirai uno obeliſco magno & excelſo di rubente petra.Et nel ſuppoſi
to quadrato uidi ĩ una facia tali hieroglyphi iſculpti.Pri-
mo in una circulare figura,una trutina,tra laquale era u-
na platina nelli triangulari,tra la trutina & il circinato dil
la platina da uno lato era uno cane,& dalaltro uno ſerpe-
diſotto laquale iaceua una antiquaria arcula,& da queſta ſubleuata reɕa era una ſpatha deteɕa,cũ lacumiato ſo
pra excedendo la trutinale lance,& quiui una corona regia intromiſſa era, gliquali cuſi io li interpretai.

IVSTITIA RECTA AMICITIA
ET ODIOEVAGINATAET NV
DA.ETPONDERATA LIBER A
LITASREGNVM FIRMITER-
SER VAT

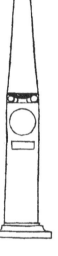

 Dapoſcia ſoto queſta in unaltra figura quadrangula uidi uno ochio,
due ſpiche di fruméto trãſuerſate ligate.Vno antiquario acinace.Poſcia
dui excuſſori di frumeto trãſuerſati tra uno cyclo & cũlorati,uno mũdo
& uno temone.Poſcia era uno ueterrimo uaſo,fora dilquale pſiliua una
fronde di elea baccata di fruɕo.Seguiua una panſa platina. due Ibide,ſei

numifmati in circo. Vno facello cum patefacta porta, cum una ara i medio. Nouiffimamente erano dui perpendiculi. Lequale figure i latino cu
fi le interpretai.

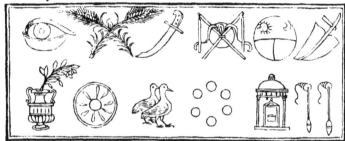

DIVO IVLIO CAESARI SEMP. AVG. TOTIVS ORB.
GVBERNAT. OB ANIMI CLEMENT. ET LIBER ALI
TATE MAEGYPTII COMMVNIA ERE.S. EREXER E.

Similmente in qualúque fron
te del recenfito fuppofito quadrato, quale la prima circulata
figura, tale unaltra fe pftaua a li
nea & ordie della prima a la de
xtra planitie dúque mirai ancora tali eleganti hieroglyphi,
primo uno uiperato caduceo.
Alla ima parte dilla uirga dil'
quale, & de qui, & deli, uidi u-
na formica che fe crefceua i ele
phanto. Verfo la fupernate æ-
qualmente dui elepháti decref
ceuano in formice. Tra quefti

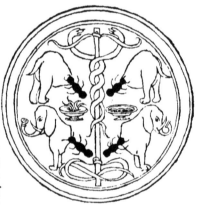

nel mediaftimo era uno uafo PACE, AC CONCORDIA PAR-
cum foco, & dalaltro lato una VAER ESCR ESCVNT, DISCOR
conchula cum aqua. cufi io li DIA MAXIMA EDECR ESCVNT.
interpretai. Pace, ac concordia
paruæ res crefcút, difcordia ma
ximæ decrefcunt.

Allincõtro di quefto era laltra circulatione. Intro laquale
mirai tale defignature di egregio expreffo. Vna ancora nel
diametrale loco tranfuerta. Sopra laquale affideua una aquila
cum le ale paffe, & nella haftu-
la ancorale intricato uno uin-
culo. foto quefti liniaméti uno
milite fedendo tra alcuni belli-
ci inftrumenti fpeculando teniua uno ferpe. Diquefto tale i-
terpreto feci.

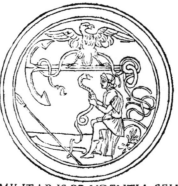

MILITARIS PRVDENTIA, SEV
DISCIPLINA IMPERII EST TE-
NACISSIMVM VINCVLVM.

Cum extrema uoluptate cõ-
templabondo quefti nobiliffi
mi concepti in tale figurato ex
preffi mirai & il quarto decon-
tra al primo circulo. Vidi uno
triumphale in la parte ima dilla
lancea, dilquale due intrafuer-
fate palme. Et item a quella cõ-
nodulate due dapfile copie fe
extolleuano. Nel mediano, da
uno lato era uno oculo, & dalaltro una ftella comete. Quefto diceua.

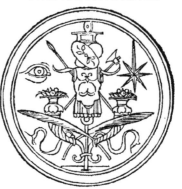

DIVIIVLII VICTORIARVMET
SPOLIORVMCOPIOSISSIMVM
TROPHAEVM, SEV INSIGNIA.

Per la magnificentia dilquale obelifco, penfai che tale non fue deue-
éto ad Thebe, ne incirco magno erecto. Dapofcia nella parte antica ritor
nando, trouai tuto difrupto il propylæo & ad lingreffo dilla diftructa por
ta iacente uidi uno frufto di trabe Zophoro, & parte dilla coronice i uno
folido i effo zophoro infcripto uidi di elegáte fcriptura di maiufcule tale dicto.

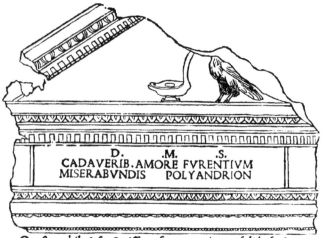

D. .M. .S.
CADAVERIB. AMORE FVRENTIVM
MISERABVNDIS POLYANDRION

Queſto nobile & ſpeƈtatiſſimo fragmento in uno ſolido fruſto anco
ra & una portiúcula dil ſuo faſtigio, o uero frontiſpicio ſe retinea egregia
méte liniato•Nella triangulare planitie dilquale dui figmenti io uidi in
ſcalpti,& non integri. Vno uolucre decapitato,arbitrai fuſſe di Bubone,
& una uetuſta lucerna, tuto di perfeƈto alabaſtryte. Cuſi io le interpretai,
VITAE LETHIFER NVNTIVS.

Peruenuto dapoſcia in la mediana parte dil tempio, alquanto ímune
& diſoccupata di freſſidine la trouai. Oue ancora il cóſumabile tempo,
ad una opera p̄clara di narrato, tuta di rubicundo porphyrite, ſolamente
hauea perdonato. Laquale era ſexangula, cum le baſe ſopra una ſolida pe
tra ophites dillamedeſima figura nel pauimento i paƈta, & ſei columnelle
diſtáte una dalaltra pedi ſei, cü lo epiſtilio. zophoro, & coronice, ſencia al
cuno liniaméto & ſigno, ma ſimplicemente terſo & puro•Gliquali erano
extrinſeco la forma imitanti. Ma interſticii in figura circinata. Oue ſopra
la piana dilla corona naſceua una cupula di unico & ſolido ſaxo, mirabi
le artificio. Laquale graciliua nel acumine, quale uno peruio infu
mibulo ſtriſſo & ſpeculare copriua una ſubterranea uacui
tate illuminata p una circulare aptione di egre
gia cancellatura impedita di metal
lina fuſura. Ilquale ſpeƈtando ci
borio di maxima pol
litura cuſi il tro
uai.

Per laquale cancellatura mirã
do maparue di fotto uedere una
certa quadratura. Per laqualcofa
accéfo di curiofa cupidine di potere ad quefta parte defcendere ri-
mabondo tra q́lle fraĉture, & mi-
nutie & ruine perquirendo qual-
che meato. Ecco che in uno mar
moreo pilone comminuto tuto
meno circa dui paffi, Inueftito di
una obftinata & flexipeda hedera
Dallaquale quafi tuta trouai occupata la pertione di una porticu
la. In laq́le da troppo fcrutario di
fio feduĉto fencia altro penficu-
lare, & inconfideratamente intra-
ui. Oue per uno cæco accliuo fca
linato defcendendo, al primo in-
greffo ma parue horrende latebre
& illumina caligine, Ma poco ftá
te affuefaĉti alquáto gli ochii cer

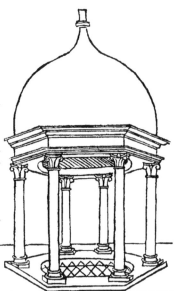

nere incominciai, & uidi uno grande & amplo loco fubterraneo cócame
rato in rotondo, & per lumido male rifonante. In columne nane fuffulto
era & fuftentato. Sene erano fubaĉte al perpendiculo dille fuperaftruĉte
dilla cupula, cum gli archi tanto loco di apertura includendo, quanto il
contento ambito delle fei fuperiore. Dallequale nane teftidunaua pofcia
tuto quefto loco candido di marmoro, di expolita quadratura decemen-
tato, & quafi non cernentife le cópaĉture. Negli quali era defputato molto A fronito, ouero Baurach. Quiui trouai il feĉticio filicato, belliffimamente expreffo, cóplanato & piano, ma fœdato di frequentia di noĉtue.
   Tra le nane era fundata foliftimo una biquadrata ara, tuta di aurical-
cho, piedi fei longa, & cum il foco & coronula alta il dimidio. Laquale era
uacua buftuariamente quale uno fepulchro. Ma nella apertione dalla fu
perficie ingiu fextante uidi una cancellatura, oueramente una crate dilla
propria materia infeme conflata. Da una facia uidi una feneftricula, penfai per quefta gli facriculi miniftrare il foco ad holocauftare la uiĉtima,
& dindi trahere il fanĉto cinere, & anchora cogitai, che fopra quella crate
poneuano incenfabondi, ouero ad adolere lanimale. Etiam fumido appa
rendo il fuffito dilla apertura. Quiui iuridicamente conieĉturai, che il fu

mo degli facrificii afcendendo fe fublimaffe per il meato dilla porphyritica cupula,& fora exalare. Et per aduentura fufpicai che il tholo, oueramente culmo mediano dil tempio fuffe aperto al rito aegyptico,& dil
fancto fumo il nidore,ouero uftrina fencia moleftare il tempio uffirfine.
Dallaltra parte dilla pdicta ara trouai di litere romane excauateexquifita
mente quefto titulo.penfai dil ara trouata da Valefio a Tarento.

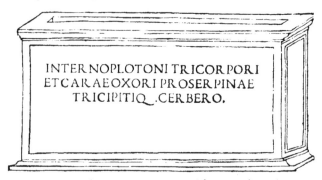

INTER NOPLOTONI TRICORPORI
ET CARAEOXORI PROSERPINAE
TRICIPITIQ .CERBERO.

In circinatione di quefto terreneo ouero fubterraneo loco,altra o patu
ra non uidi finon appacti fedili dilla propria materia . Tute quefte cofe
cum grande & fmifurato piacere, & fingular deuotione diligentemente
mirate di fopra ritornai.Oue mirabondo dilla integritate di quefta ifigne
opatura di ciborio. Tra me confirmai il fufpecto,che il cielo dil tempio
aperto fi fuffe.Impero che la ruina incircuito era aggerata,& quefta parte
trouai immune.Hora quiui infpectando moffi gli ochii,& uidi una tribuna alquanto integra.Difubito cum gli ochii comitanti gli pedi, ad ql-
la feftino andai. Nel cielo dillaquale una artificiofa pictura era iui rima-
fta cum incredibile conato & efficientia dillartifice di opera colorifica di
mufeaco fubtilmente expreffa.

Quiui cauernatamente picto era uno fornice di fpiffa caligine infu-
fcato monftrante una ingente & trifta, & terricula fpelunca tuta cariofa
quale uno multicauo ouero fiftulofo pumice.Laqle dallato finiftro uerfo la medioftima parte uicino ad una afperrima inua,& ferruginea & có
fragofa rupe terminaua. Nellaqle fe uideua uno hiato di concauatura di
nanti,&nella facia uerfo il fuo finire diftante da uno tofineo faxeo monte
fcrupeo & chaimeno.Quefto per il medefimo modo incauernato allincontro & puro• Nella mediata altecia tra luno & laltro traiectaua uno bi
partito ponte di ferro candente fina al mediato & pofcia apparea frigo-
riffimo

riſſimo metallo. Oltra queſti pendicei & puttrei ſaxi, per quella diuiſione
tra uno & laltro, ſi dimóſtraua intro eſſere tutto ardeſcente loco di ſoco
pieno di ignite & uolante ſcintille diſcurréte, & cane ſauille cadéte(quali
denſiſſimi atomi negli radii ſolari)crepitanti p le ſiáme ſincto ſolertemé
te & uno ignito laco bulliéte, & molti ſpiraṁti extuarii p li ſaxi apparédo
  Dalla parte antica uno ſcuro & cretamoſo laco glaciale & rigidiſſimo
dimonſtrantiſe. Et dallato dextro ancora uno crepidinoſo & ruuido &
muriceo monte era, & di colore ſulphureo. Per ilquale in diuerſi hiaticu-
li uomeua tetro & caliginoſo ſumo. Quale di materia repugnante alin-
greſſo dillactiuo ſoco, & imediate ſcaturiente una ſuppurata materia igni
ta. Laq́le uomitióe daua uiſta di crepitare, o uero ſare ſcloppo, Quale ua-
pore concreto diffuſamente exalare coacto, & poſcia negli ſiſtuloſi mea-
ti il ructo ritornare, Et quella dimonſtratione che uno loco nó ſaceua lal
tro loco ad idicare ſuppliua. In q́ſto era una ſcabra ruptura cauaméte in-
ſpeluncata cú crude graue & auerne ombre. Nellaquale foſſura era impac-
to tenaro cú una ænea porta ruuidaméte exacta in q́ſto arſo & punico-
ſo ſaxo. Et quiui ſotto q́ſti cauernacei curuamini & crepidie triſauce cer
bero inſomne ſedente di pilatura nigerrimo & humecto, capitato di ſpauentoſi ſerpi, di aſpecto horrendo & terribile, cú graue afflato quelle me-
talline ualue in ſopito explorabondo cú inconniua uigilia, in perpetua
luce le pupule excubante.
  In queſto horrendo & cuſpidinoſo littore & miſerrimo ſito dil algen-
te & ſetoriſico laco, ſtaua la ſæuiente Teſiphone efferata & crudele cú il ui
perino capillaméto. i le meſchine & miſerrime anime, iplacabiléméte fu-
ribonda. Leq́le cadeuano cateruaméte nello æternalméte rigidiſſimo laco giu dal ſerreo ponte, & rotátiſe p le algéte onde ſugire properáte il penoſo & mortiſero algore, puemuano al ſrigidiſſimo littore. Et uſcite iſœlice & ſugitiue dala tartarea ſuria, p ſopra una difficillima, laborioſa, & ſa-
lebricoſa ripa, alla ſiniſtra mano, Fugiuano citule cú le ſauce apte, & cú le
ciglie depreſſe, & cú gli rubéti & lachrymoſi ochii indicáte clamori, ſtri-
dore di ſauce, & cú doloroſi piáti & guai. Leq́le oppreſſe & di horrore una
cú laltra ipulſe, & icóculcantiſe giu nel ſrigidiſſimo auerno & pfundo, ir
ruéte pcipitauaſe. Et q́lle che del pcipitio euadeuano, nella ſcabra cauer-
na ſe ricótrauano in laltra horribile ſuria di Megæra, & phibiua che q́lle
in le uoláte ſiáme nó ſe pcipitaſſeron. Et coacte ſopra lo icendioſo ponte
ſaliuano. Tale penoſo ordine iudicai eſſere dalaltra parte, pche la luctiſi
ca Alecto ſorore dille due noiate di Acheronte ſiliole & dilla tetra nocte,
& eſſa era obſtaculo & furialméte ipediua, che lalme deputate alle ſempi-
terne ſiáme nó obrueſſeron nel laco rigente. Ma iſpauétate dalla horren-
da ſuria ſaliuano & eſſe, cú le altre obuiátiſe, il biaſtemato ponte. Et cuſi

q

appareua ad me,che lanime che allardente incendio, dãnate erano , nel
giacio demigrare optauano,& quelle che adiudicate furono al torpen-
tiſſimo laco,molto piu chel ſtyge palude frigidiſſimo , exceſſiuamente
deſiderauano nelle maledicte & calorifice fláme recentabonde intrare.
Ma ſforciate di ſalire il fallace traiecto.Il candeſcente paſſo,per fatale diſ
poſitione ſe diuideua per tale modo,Che lanime ,pſcripte allo inextin-
guibile foco,iterũ cadeuano nel ſuo æternalmente conſtituito loco.Per
il ſimigliante quelle che lo ineuitabile algore perfuge tentauano di eua-
dere,erano dal ponte nel rigentiſſimo profundo reſũmerſe. Per uirtute
dapoſcia dilla diuina iuſtitia il tranſito al ſuo priſtino eſſere ritornaua.

Sencia iteruallo altre doloroſe alme q̃ſto ,pprio ſucceſſiuamẽte atten
tauano,cũ uano & i cõpote uoto,& per niuno modo cõſequire ualeuano il deſiderato effecto. Quelle miſerrime anime dunq̃ che feſtinauão
ſenza quietefugire,da furioſo horrore & rabie agitate,le icendioſe fláme
& per ſolleuamẽto uenire & refrigerarſe nel giacio nõ poteão. Et q̃lle ſi-
milmẽte che dauano aſſidua opera di fugire il duriſſimo fredo,& intrare nelle ardẽte fláme fruſtrate dil maximo diſio nõ ualeuano . Et q̃ſta ad
quelle gliera ieffugibile & pœna ideſinente,ſemp piu deſideroſe perden
do omni ſperáza.Laquale táto piu ardẽte auiditate accreſceuão , quáto
che ſopra il põte luna & laltra ſentiuano,quelle dil ardore il reflexo dil
ſuo fredo,Et q̃lle gelate, il calore,luno cũ laltro obuiátiſe nel ſuo termi-
ne.Et queſto nel affecto era maxima uegetatione di pœna & di tormẽto.
Per laquale coſa,cũ tanta obſtinata arte di coloramẽto & di ſimulati geſti & expreſſi conati,uidi tale pictura fabrefacta,& exquiſitamente perfe
cta,quanto mai fare ſi potrebbe & dimonſtrare.Et il titulo indicante era
inſcripto.Che nelle urente fláme erano cõdénate le anime che per trop
po foco damore,ſe medeſime occideuão.Et nel horrido gelo,quelli erano demerſi,che rigidi & fredolenti allo Amore & renuenti ſe haueuano
obſtinatamẽte præſtati.Finalmẽte cum tale diſpoſitiõe mirai q̃ſto odio-
ſo,ſpauenteuole & euitando Barathro,Che doue gli lachi ſe ricontraua
no,cioe il frigorifico,cũ lardétiſſimo,p la cõtrarietate fare doueuano cũ
æterna cõtrouerſia uno terribile tonare,pche poſcia obuii ſe imergeua-
no ambi dui i abrupto ,pcipitio effuſi i ſcuro uaſto &pfundiſſimo meato & imẽſo abyſſo.Oue era la ,pfunditate tanto artificioſamẽte dallartifi
ce ficta,che per la coloratione quelle dimonſtratione eſſere uere menti-
uano,& di uidere una abſorbentiſſima uoragine , Cum mirifica æmula
tione di gli coloramenti.Et di ſymmetria liniale di proſpecto,& dille fi
gure la elegantia,& copioſo inuento,& artifica deſignatione,& cum incredibile argutia,Che Parrhaſio Epheſio inſigne pictore unque primo
diſimile excogitato non pote gloriarſe.

Dunque

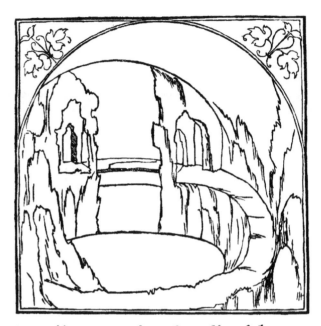

Dunque chi accuratamente tale expreſſura conſideraua facilmente conieĉturare cuſi eſſere il poteua, per che il faĉtore di ſolertia uberrimo , & di cogitato p̄ſtante, hauea quiui exquiſitamente finĉto le anime ad expreſſo corporale. Lequale umbre non poſſino apparere ſe non concreto aere & condenſato in quella effigie, p laquale lo effeĉto ſi comprenda. Et pero molte anime lorechie obturantiſe, altre non audeuano (copertoſi cum le palmule gliochii) riguardare nel terrifico & gurgitale abyſſo, pieno di ſpauenteuoli, terribili, & uarii monſtri, altre pallide ad exprimere il torpente fredo cum le brace al peĉto ſtringentiſſe, alcune adimonſtrare lardore flauano fumido ſpirito, altre ad indicare la mœrente triſtitia, & doloroſa pena, gli digiti dille mane impeĉtine giunĉti piangeuano. Onde ſopra il limitato ponte nella compaĉtura diagonale cateruamente occurſantiſe luna & laltra dille prime arietaua, & non ualeuano procedere, per la con culcatione dille ſequente. Allhora il ponte per ordine fatale ſempiterno ſeparatoſe reiiciendo le proprie nel proprio loco ritornaua, & incolato, & iterg̃ coniugato altre indefinente attentauano, ſucceſſiuamente quello

q ii

ſcandendo.Dique lanime doloroſe diſperate optando la horrifica mor
te,molto piu che gli ſpauentoſi lochi & horrende furie abhorriuano , che
epſa odibile morte uanamente affectata.Ilquale iſœlice & fœtuléto here‹
bo era cuſi códucto & depolito,che ancora ad gli iſpectori non exile ſpa
uento iduceua.

In queſto loco uidi una quadrata ara,Nella facia ouero fronte dilla‐
quale di maiuſcule pfecte queſto titulo trouai inſcripto .

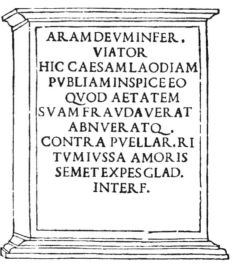

```
ARAMDEVMINFER.
     VIATOR
HIC CAESAMLAODIAM
PVBLIAMINSPICEEO
QVOD AETATEM
SVAM FRAVDAVERAT
ABNVERATQ.
CONTRA PVELLAR.RI
TVMIVSSA AMORIS
SEMETEXPESGLAD.
  INTERF.
```

Molto lætificato diqui partitome,tra le ruine uno nobile ſaxo di mar
moro quadrato trouai,in uno lato fracto,ma la magiore parte riſeruata i
uno fronte tra le undulature nel medio,i modo di due quadrágulette cũ
larco era introſcalpto,& dequi,& deli, una figura altiuſcula ouola, luna
hauea.D.& uno capo di larua,& laltra uno.M.& unaltro capo
il cimatio alquáto faſtigiato,ma de cacuminato,ouei
fixo uno ueterrimouaſo æneo promineua ſen‐
cia operculo hiante,penſai i quello fuſſe‐
ron le cinere códite,cum tale iſcri‐
ptione.il reſiduo di linia‐
menti immu‐
ne.

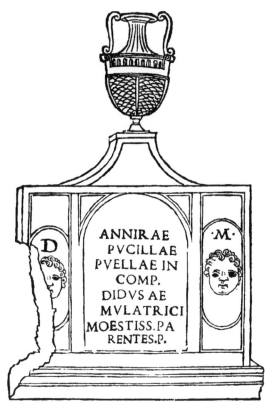

ANNIRAE
PVCILLAE
PVELLAE IN
COMP.
DIDVS AE
MVLATRICI
MOESTISS.PA
RENTES.P.

Proximo a quefto foliftimo iacente,uidi & quefto elegante epitaphio, in
una tabula prophyrica,p laquale effere ftato uno fupbo fepulchro cóie-
cturai.Per che ad gli ambi lateri,continua per fractura appareua,& nó cu
fi tabula fimplice.Ma quefta parte pura di liniamenti conftaua
immune,cum la literatura relicta.circa ilquale ger
minoe la nafturcia hiberida.

q   iii

```
        D.                    .M.
   GLADIATORI MEO AMORE CV
   IVS EXTREME PER VST A
   INMOR T. LAGVOREM DECVB.
   AT EIVS CRVORE HEV ME MISE
   RAM IMPIATA CONV ALVI. D.
         FAVST.AVG.
   PIE MONVMENT. RELINQVENS
   VT.Q. ANN.SANG. TVRTVR.IN
   TER SACRIFICAND. ARC.RELIG.
   HANC INTINGIEX.L IX ACCEN.
   FACVL.ET COLLACHRYMVLAN
   TES PVELLAE SOLVERENTVR
   LVCTVMQ. FVNERAL. OBTAN
   TI INDICIVM DOLORIS DE VEL
   LAT.CRINIB.PROMISSIS RVSSA
   RENT PECTORA FACIEMQ. DI
   EM INTEGRVM PROPITIATIS
   MAN.CIRCA SEPVLCRVM SATA
   GERENT ANNV ALITER
       PERPETVO REPE
          TVND.
       EX.T.    F.I.
```

Dapofcia che io hebbi quefti dui epitaphii accuratamente perlecti,
&gratiffimamente uifi,folicito iquirente riuoluédo gli ochii,ecco chio
uedo una fepultura hiftoriata. Allaquale fencia pigritare andai. i la par
te áteriore dillaquale appacta era una arula, iſeme cú tali expreffi. Sopra
la piana di effa di miro artificio impofito era uno capo di filuano capro
ne,retéto per uno degli corni da uno feniculo,cum la tefta di capigli al
ᵗmodo uetufto tormentati cófufi.il quale era iduto fopra il nudo dipa ⸗
lio reiecto fopra la fpalla dextra,fottouia uenendo dalla finiftra ritornã
do fopra la dextra,& nel tergo dependulo proximo egli era di pelle ca⸗
prina ueftito,una antica,& laltra poftica al dorfo,fopra gli hume
ri,gli pedi di ambedue le pelle innodati,& gli altri tra le
coxe pendenti cum il ruuido pelo alla carne uol
tato,& cinctofi di una torque,ouero ftro⸗
phio facto di tamo,ouero uite ni⸗
gra,cum le foglie
fue.

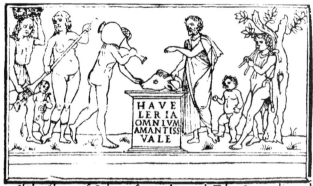

Ilqle cũ le tumefacte bucce fonaua due rurale Tibie, & appodiato ad
uno torofo trunco di Dendro cæfo, da uetuſtate tuto uacuo, cum peruie
crepature & rami difeoli rarii & folii, Cum il capillaméto incompto &
in frondato. Tra queſti dui faltaua uno puello nudo. Dalaltro lato era
uno, che fopra gli robuſti humeri, uno Armillo futile baiulante lo orificio inuerfo fopra il cornigero capo il mero fpargeua. Achoſta egli era
una matrona, cum il capillamento demiſſo decapillata, & queſta & il ua
ſtafo dilarmillo nudi, & lachrymabonda. Tenendo una facula cum la
parte accenfa in giu. Tra queſti dui appareua uno Satyrulo puero, ilqua
le nelle mano uno ferpe molto inuoluto ſtringeua. Sequiua pofcia una
ˉuricola uetula canifera, fopra il nudo induta di panno uolante, fopra gli fianchi cincta. Del capo inconcinno fopra il caluato, hauea uno ceſticillo, & di fopra portaua una uiminea ciſta pie
na di frucſti & di fronde & nelaltra mano uno uaſo te
niua dilorificio oblongo cretaceo. Queſte figure optimamente erano infcalpte & afpe-
ramente. In larula cuſi era infcripto. Ex
citato fummo pere da tanta uenu-
ſtate di monuméti quæritabon
do, ad me uno elegantiſſimo
in uno faxo infcripto epi
taphio Romano tale
iucundiſſimo dia-
logo fe offerite &
tali cũ ornaméti.

* * *

q iiii

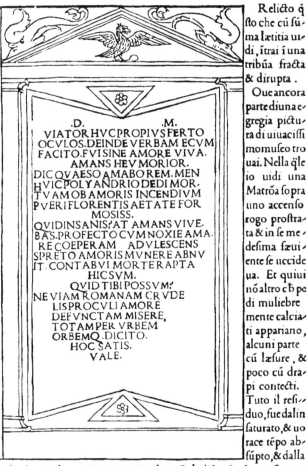

Relicto q̃
sto che cū sū
ma lætitia ui-
di, ītrai ī una
tribūa fracta
& dirupta.
Que ancora
parte diuna e-
gregia pictu-
ra di uiuaciſſi
momuſeo tro
uai. Nella q̃le
io uidi una
Matrōa ſopra
uno accenſo
rogo proſtra-
ta & in ſe me-
deſima ſæui-
ente ſe uccide
ua. Et quiui
nō altro cb pe
di muliebre
mente calcia-
ti appariano,
alcuni parte
cū læſure, &
poco cū dra-
pi contecti.
Tuto il reſi-
duo, fue dal in
ſaturato,& uo
race tēpo ab-
ſūpto,& dalla

antiquitate,& da uenti,& piogie & ardente Sole diſtructo, In queſto medeſimo loco la Area era cōminuta,& il maiore fruſto,era q̃ſto riuerſo cū
tale ſcriptura ridriciātilo io il trouai. Proximo a q̃ſto ſoliſtimo iacéte di
petra alabaſtrite,trouai uno antiq̃rio uaſo,alto piu di uno & ſemipaſſo.
cū una dille anſe friata,&pte fracto nella ſua corpulétia fina alla aptura
parte Supaſſideua uno ſemi cubo, o uero Taxillo,alto pede uno,o uero
palmi

palmi q̃tro. Nelq̃le in una facie, dal fróte dila fractura era iscripto, & similméte oue era rupto p idicio di alcune litere pte fragmétate, & ítegre, parte rimaste. Poscia nella subiécta corpulétia dalla circinante cinctura uerso el fondo, nellaquale erano appacte le anse, nel fronte dilla fractura era questa præstante scriptura.

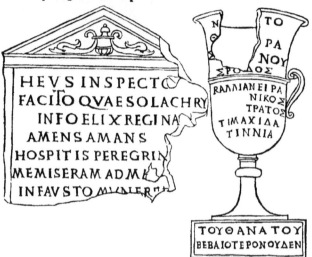

HEVS INSPECTO
FACITO QVAE SO LACHRY
INFOELIX REGINA
AMENS AMANS
HOSPITIS PEREGRI
MEMISERAM ADME
IN FAVSTO MVLIER

N TO
PA
NOY
ΣΡΟΔΟΣ
RAΛΛIANEI PA
NIKOΣ
TPATOΣ
TIMAXIΔA
TINNIA

TOYΘANATOY
BEBAIOTEPON OYΔEN

Re licti questi rupti monumenti, ad una destructa tribuna deueni nellaquale alquanto fragmento di museaco si comprendeua. Oue picto mirai uno homo affligente una damicella. Et uno naufragio. Et uno adolescétulo sopra il suo dorso equitante una fanciulla, nataua ad uno littore deserto. Et parte uedeuasi di uno leone. Et quegli dui in una nauicula remiganti. Il sequente distructo. Et ancora questa parte era in molti lochi lacerata, Non ualeua intendere totalmente la historia. Ma nel pariete crustato marmoreo, era intersepta una tabula ænea, cum maiuscule græcæ. Tale epigramma inscripto hauea. Ilquale nel proprio Idiomate in táta pietate me prouocaua legendo si miserando caso, che di lachryme contenirme non potui, dánando la rea fortuna. Ilquale sæpicule perlegendo, quanto io ho potuto cusi il fece latino.

HEV SVIATOR PAVLVLVM INTERSERE. MANIB. ADIV
RAT. PRODITVM. AC LEGENS POLYSTONOS METAL
LO OSCVLA DATO ADDENS . AH FORTVNAE CRVDE
LE MONSTRVM VIVERE DEBVISSENT. LEONTIA PVEL
LA LOLII INGENVI ADVLESCENT . PRIMARIA AMORIS
CVM INTEMPERIE VRGERET . PATERNIS AFFECTA
CRVCIATVB. A VFVGIT. INSEQVIT. LOL. SED INTER AM
PLEXANDVM A PYRATIS CAPTI INSTITORI CVIDAM
VENDVNT. AMBO CAPTIVI NAVEM ASCEND. CVM NO
CTVSIBILEONT. LOL. A VFERRI SVSPICARET. ARREP
TO GLADIO NAVTAS CVNCTOS TRVCIDAT. NAVIS
ORTA MARIS SAEVIT. SCOPVL. TERRAM PROPE COL
LISAMERGIT. SCOPVL. ASCEND. FAMIS IMPVLSVLE
ONT. HVMERIS ARRIPIENS IMPONO. FAVE ADES DVM
NEDT. PATER INQVIENS. NOS NOSTRAMQ. FORT. TI
BI COMMITTO. TVNC DELPHINEO NIXV BRACHIIS SE
CO VNDVLAS, AT LEONT. INTERNATANDVM ALLO
QVIT. SVM NE TIBI MEA VITA MOLESTIAE? TIPVLA LE
VIOR LEONT. CORCVLVM, ATQ. SAEPICVLE ROGANS
SVNT NETIBI VIRES MEA SPES. MEA ANIMVLA? AIO.
EAS EXCITAS, MOX COLLVM AMPLEXATA ZACHARI
TER BAIVLANTEM DEOSCVLAT. SOLAT. HORTAT.
VRINANTEMINANIMAT, GESTIO, AD LITT. TANDEM
DEVENIM. SOSPITES. INSPERATO INFREMENS LEO, AG
GREDITVR, AMPLEXAMVR INVICEM, MORIBVNDIS
PARCIT LEO. TERRITI CASV, NAVICVLAM LITTORI V
NA CVM REMIGA LIPAL MICVLA DEIECTAM FVGITIVI
ASCEN. VTERQ. ALTERNATIM CANTANTES REMIGA
MVS. DIEM NOCTEMQ. TERTIAM ERRANT. IPSVM
TANTVM VNDIQ. COELVM PATET. LETHALI CRVCIA
MVR FAME ATQ. DIVTINA IN EDIA TABESCENTIB.
R VIMVS IN AMPLEXVS, LEONTIA INQVIENS AMABO
FAME PERIS? SATTECVM ESSE LOLI DEPASCOR, AST IL
LA SVSPIRVLANS MI LOLI DEFICIS? MINIME INQVAM
AMORE SED CORPORE, SOLIS VIBRANTIBVS ET MV
TVIS LINGVIS DEPASCEBAMVR DVLCITER, STRICTI
VSQ. BVCCIS HIANTIBVS OSCVLISS VAVE INIECTIS HE
DERACITER AMPLEXABAMVR, AMBO ASTROPHIA
MORIMVR, PLEMMYRIIS NEC SAEVIENTIB. HVC AVRA
DEVEHIMVR, AC AERE QV AEST VARIO MISERI IPSIS IN
NEXI AMPLEXV B. MANES INTER PLOTONICOS HIC SI
TISVMVS, QVOSQ. NON RETINVIT PYRATICA
RAPACITAS NEC VORAVIT LEONIA IN
GLVVIES, PELAGIQ. IMMENSITAS
ABNVIT CAPERE, HVIVS VRNVLAE
ANGVSTIA HIC CAPIT AMBOS,
HANC TE SCIRE VOLEBAM
INFOELICITATEM.
VALE.
* *
*

De qui partitome piu auidamente luſtrãdo p le aceruate ruine, trouai unaltra ara tetragona. Laquale nella ſua plana haueua una baſi ſencia Plintho, cioe una gula, dapoſcia una faſceola, & dapoi uno thoro. Oltra q̃ſto era æquato. Nellaquale æquatura aſſideua uno plitho, ouero lataſtro, che da angulo ad angulo faceua uno ſinuato, quarto uno dilla ſua figura quadrata incuruantiſſe paulatine. La proiectura degli quali anguli non excedeua la circũferẽtia dil totque, ouero thoro ſubiecto. Sopra il quale abbacato plitho iaceua uno circulare fũdo duno uaſo. La circũſtãtia dilq̃le nõ præteriua lo exito degli anguli dil ſubacto plintho. Il quale uaſo ſe dilataua tanto nella apertione, quanto era lo extremo delinfino dilla ſuppoſita gula dilla baſi. Lo orolo o uero labro dilquale ſeruã do la ſua craſſitudine ren deua uno inflexo i ſe me- deſimo inuertiſcente, nel la ara uidi tale epigrãma.

Indi partentime io tro uai uno nobile fragmẽto di optimo porphyrite, cũ dui capi equini ſcalpti. Dagliquali quali una in plicata ligatura, dui rami di myrto intraſuerſati, & penduli retinente uſciua. Nel medio dil tranſuerſo erano cum una ſtringien te cimoſa di mira factura innodati. Tra uno & laltro oſſo ſopra le myrtee fronde uidi di belliſſime ionice maiuſcule tale ſcriptura. il reſto dilla ſcriptura cum la petra diſtructo.

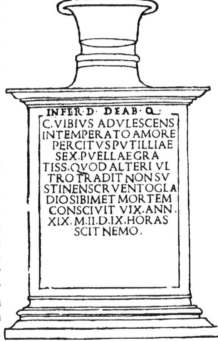

INFER·D·DEAB·Q̃·
C·VIBIVS ADVLESCENS
INTEMPERATO AMORE
PERCITVSPVTILLIAE
SEX·PVELLAEGRA
TISS·QVOD ALTERI VL
TRO TRADIT NON SV
STINENSCRVENTOGLA
DIO SIBIMET MORTEM
CONSCIVIT VIX·ANN·
XIX·M·II·D·IX·HORAS
SCIT NEMO·

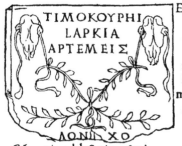

Excitato fummopere da tanta ue
nuftate di monumenti indaga-
bondo, ad me uno epigramma
alquantulo perplexo candido
in marmoro trouai, folamente
la parte infcripta di una arula ri
mafta. il refiduo confracto in ter
ra iaceua.

Cú maxima delectatione & piacere quefti fpectandi fragmenti mi
rando, auido piu anchora indagá-
te altro di nouo trouare. Dindi dúque qual animale quæritabódo il
pabulo fempre piu grato non altra
mente tranfferendome per gli agge
ri di ruine di ingenti frufti di colúne, & tale integre. Dil lequale uolen
do fapere la forte, una menfuarai al
folo extéfa, & dal focco fina alla có
tractura, trouai dil fuo fcapo la pce
rità feptéo diametro dilla fua ima
craffitudine Quiui pximo mi fe of
ferfe uno ueterrimo fepulchro, fen
cia alcuna fcriptura, nellaquale per
una fractura rimando uidi folo le
funerale ueftimenti, & calciamenti
petrificati. Coniecturai ragioneuol
mente dilla petra farcophago (per tale effecto) di troade di Afia, fufpicádo
dil cadauero di Dario.

D.   M.
LYNDIA THA
SIVS PVELLA
PVER HIC SVM
SINE VIVERE
NOLVI MORI
MALVI
AT SINORIS
SATEST
✳VALE✳

Et ad uicino uidi uno nobile fepulchro di porphyrite, exquifitamente excalpto tra filuatichi arbufcoli, dilquale mi fe offerfe ad le-
gere uno elegante epitaphio, & hauea il coopertorio in tem
plo egregio, & fcandulato fquameamente, una parte
dil dicto fopra larca riftato, & laltra iaceua
deiecta foliftima, & di tale
præftante titulo in-
fcripto.

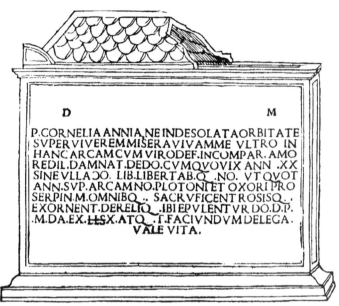

D   M

P.CORNELIA ANNIA.NE INDESOLATA ORBITATE
SVPER VIVEREM MISERA VIVAMME VLTRO IN
HANC ARCAM CVM VIRO DEF.INCOMPAR. AMO
REDIL.DAMNAT.DEDO.CVM QVO VIX ANN .XX
SINE VLLA ⊃O. LIB.LIBERTAB.Q .NO. VT QVOT
ANN.SVP.ARCAM NO.PLOTONI ET OXORI PRO
SERPIN.M.OMNIBQ .. SACRVFIÇENT ROSISQ .
EXORNENT.DERELIQ. .IBI EPVLENT VR DO.D.P.
.M.DA.EX.H.SX.ATQ .T.FACIVNDVM DELEGA.
VALE VITA.

Sotto ancora (de q partitomi) di una corymbifera & errante hedera
da uno deroſo alamento di muro propendula, molto di fronde denſa,
uno ſpeċtabile zygaſtrion aſſideua di una petra alleboro ſimigliante, fin
allhora nella maiore parte ancora terſa & luculea. Détro laq̃le curioſam
te riguardádo per una fixura, o uero rima dil cooptorio plano dui cada
ueri integri riſeruati. p laquale coſa dritaĩnte arbitrai che di ſaxo chemi
tes era queſto ſepulchro. Nel frôte dilquale uidi queſti hieroglyphi ægy
ptici iſculpto, & itro ancora molte ampulle di uitro & molte figulinate
di terra, & alcune ſtaticule archæo more agyptitio & una antiquaria lu
cerna di metallo artificioſamente faċta , & nel ſuffito dil tegumé
to pendice, quella una catenula illaqueata retinente ſuſpen
ſa ardeua, et proximo alla teſta degli ſepulti era
no due coronule. Lequale coſe auree iu
dicai, ma per il tempo, & per il lucernale fumo iſuſcate. tale
fue la interpreta-
tione.

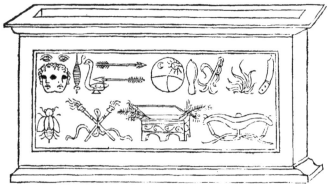

DIIS MANIBVS MORS VITAE CONTRARIAET VELO
CISSIMA CVNCTA CALCAT.SVPPEDITAT. RAPIT
CONSVMIT. DISSOLVIT .MELLIFLVE DVOS MVTVO
SE STRICTIM ET ARDENTER AMANTES, HIC EXTIN
CTOS CONIVNXIT.

Lætificato cum incredibile folacio, per tanta uarietate di antiquarie ,&
magnifice opere,ancora fencia dubio mi accrefceua lanimo infaciabil‐
mente piu luftrabondo altre nouitate iueftigare.Dique & fi prima lachry
mabondo me excitaua lo epitaphio græco degli dui miferabili amati di
iedia mortui,molto piu etiam mi fe aprefentoe uno fpectatiffimo, ma mi
ferando monumento,di dualtri infœliciffimi amanti,in uno magno fa‐
xo extante,cum tale liniamento expreffo. Vno quadrato per il
diagonio fubleuato,cótiniua in fe dui pillaftrelli
cú una coronula & femihemicyclo di‐
fopra.Tragliqli,dagli anguli dillar
culo propédeua una tabella, nel
laquale legiendo uidita
le miferofo epigram‐
ma.

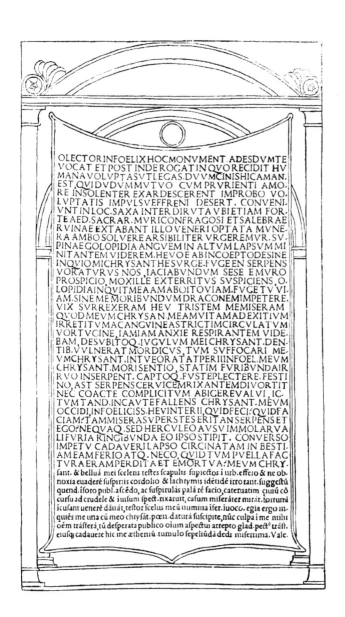

Lecto il cópaſſioneuole caſo degli ſfortunati amanti di q̃ſto pſtantiſ
ſimo epigráma. De qui ancora ſũme contento partitome, nó molti paſſi
facédo mi occorſe una nobile tabula di marmoro tetragona, cum alq̃to
di faſtigio, Cum due colũnelle una per lato. de diſegno imune & expedite. Et per il capto di tutto il quadrágulo era quaſi euulſa una foliata co
rona, o uero gioia, diligentemente conducta. Nella quale io legi tale in-
ſcriptione. Laquale petra in terra deiecta iaceua. Ma cum la operatura ſu
pina. Lequale elegante uarietate nó poco piacere nelanimo mio iucun-
damente accumulauano.

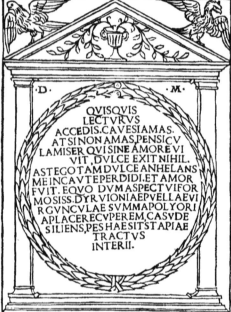

QVISQVIS
LECTVRVS
ACCEDIS. CA VESIAMAS.
AT SI NON AMAS, PENSI CV
LA MISER QVI SINE AMORE VI
VIT, DVLCE EXIT NIHIL.
ASTEGO TAM DVLCE ANHELANS
ME INCAVTE PERDIDI. ET AMOR
FVIT. EQVO DVM ASPECTVI FOR
MOSISS. DYR VIONIAE PVELLAE VI
RGVNCVLAE SVMMA POLYORI
A PLACERE CVPEREM, CASV DE
SILIENS, PES HAESIT ST AP IAE
TRACTVS
INTERII.

IN REM TVAM MATVRE PROPERA. VALE.

Piu ardente-
mete inuaſo me
trouaua ad la in
ueſtigatióe dille
digniſſime ope
átiq̃rie, mi ſapre
ſentoe una diſru
pta tribũa, cũ ri-
ſeruato pariete
dextro, Nelq̃le
uidi cũ exceſſi-
ua uoluptate, u-
no porphyriti-
co ſepulchro, di
excogitato di-
gniſſimo , & di
opatura excellé-
tiſſimo, & de ipé
ſa mirabile, & di
artificio di ſcul-
ptura ícredibile.
Ilq̃le cóſtaua, ne
li extremi lateri
excitato da due
colũnelle q̃drá-
gule, uno ſuo ter
tio exacte, cũ regulate ſtrie, Sopra uno pedamto cũ la b aſi collocate, Et a
ppédiculo ſubiecta era una arula, cũ tre elegáte nymphe luctuoſe uerſo
il mediáo cóuerſe collachrymauáo. p il ſimile dal altro lato, ſemidi uulſe
dal ſolido, nó ſéza li correlarii & req̃ſiti lini iámti. Sopra li ábi capitelli lo
epiſtylio ornato ſe extédeua. Poi cóuoluti di uenuſtiſſime fronde & fiori
inueſtito

inueſtito. il zophoro ſopra reſideua locato,di cõdecente coronula cop∕
to. Tra luna & laltra quadrangula alquanto,uno ſolio,o uero nichio ,cũ
regulata excauatura deſtria promíneua,adlibella dil piano, tra eſſe qua-
drangule. La prominétia dilquale faceua,dauno & laltro lato dilla ſua ap
tione unopilaſtrello, cú capitelli & baſe.Sopra gliquali ſaliua una trabe∕
inflexa.Tanto diuulſi dal æquato,ouero piano, che reſtaua nella interio
re parte,cioe ad gli labri dil ſolio,uno lingello. Adlibella degli capitelli,
cingeua el ſolio,uno undulato illigaméto,& diſopra la hemicupula.

Gliquali pilaſtrelli egregiamente erano di ſcalptura ornati . Sotto gli
pilaſtrelli iaceua una piecta arula altiuſcula,cũ gli ornati degli ſopra ſtã
ti pilaſtrelli.Tra una & laltra proiectura dille dicte arule,ouero ſubcolũ
nio,io uidi una iſcriptione græca,perlaquale conobi eſſere queſto il mo∕
numento dilla pia regina diCaria,cuſi diceua. ΑΡΤΕΜΙΣΙΔΟΣ ΒΑ-
ΣΙΛΙΔΟΣ ΣΡΟΔΟΝ. Cum ſochi, & coronette,& ſime,& gulule, opti
mamente il tuto cincto & ſotiale.

Nel piano inferiore dil nichio era uno plintho dilla narrata materia i
aſpecto belliſſime deornato di ſcalptura,ſopra la plana dilquale affixe ſta
uano quatro æquilocate gramfie di leõe di metallo iaurato. Gliquali p∕
meua una antiquaria arcula,cum liniamenti di expreſſo inſigne. Sopra
il tectorio era uno ſcãno , per il capto dilla copertura,fincto di panno ſe
riceo contecto,cum ambiente fimbriatura.

Sedeua ſopra una matrona Regina,cum regio culto,& maieſtale ídu∕
mento,nel pecto fibulato ſopra una aſſettata ueſtitura.Laquale dal colla∕
rio in giu per il pecto,& tranſuerſariamente nel cingiere circundaua una
faſceola,& ſopra il uentre dilatata i forma di tetraphila,cioe in una figura
di quatro hemicycli. Nellaquale di maiuſcule græce era cuſi annotato.
ΜΑΥΣΩΛΕΙΟΝ ΑΤΙΜΗΤΟΝ.

Cum la dextera teniua uno calice alla bucca potabonda , & nelaltra
teniua una uirgula,ouero ſceptro cum gli effuſi capigli ,ſopra il capo cir
cumplexi duna corona alquanto faſtigiata, adunaltra corolla nella cer∕
uice acuminata.Dallaquale concinamente,& pectinata deſcendeua la ca
pilatura.

Sopra il cuneo dil trabe arcuato promineua una ouola figura cõpla∕
nata di altecia fina ſotto alla proiectura dilla ſima dilla coronice. Nellaq
le mirai í preſſa una facie di regia maieſtate coronata cum barba prolixa,
& la cæſarie intorta. Arbitrai fuſſe il uero ſimulachro dil marito. Retinu
ta dequi & deli da dui nudi ſpiritelli alati , ſopra lo extremo circinao dil∕
la trabe arcuata ſedenti.

Gliquali cũ laltre mane ſolute,extéto il brachiolo,una cordicella ænea

r

teniuano propédula ícuruata. Perlaquale demigrati erano alcuni ballu-
ſti. Et dalla retinente mano perpendicularmente teniuano penſile uno fi
lo rameo ſyrmato & ibaccato, tuti optime inaurati.

Sopra la plana dilla corona proclinato alquanto aſcédeua uno plítho,
cũ multiplici ornati. Nella ſua plana nel mediano anteriore reſideua una
rotũdatione di metallo. Laquale inconcluſo hauea una nigerrima petra,
ancora ſpeculare. In laquale uidi tale ſcriptura di maiuſcule grœce EPΩ
ΤΟΣ ΚΑΤΟΠΤΡΟΝ. Il labro ambiente di metallo uno palmo di latitudine coœǫ̃ta uenuſtamente era bullato. Nel ſupremo circinato ſuo re-
ǎ ſtaua una perfeǎa imagine nuda dilla materia metallina inaurata, cũ
la dextera tenete una haſtula, & ne laltra uno antiquario clypeo, di egregio liniaméto inſcalpto, Da uno & laltro lato di queſta rotundatiõe, uno
dequi & laltro deli. Cũ il dorſo appodiati ſedenti ſopra la piana dui alati
puelli, uerſo le proieǎure una facola accenſa teniuano.

Nel cliuo dil plintho ſopranarrato ſimilmente cum, il dorſo ſeden-
do erano dui nudi infantuli & alati, ſopra la plana dilla corona, cũ le ma
ne iconſpeǎo retiniuano uno pomulo, & cũ li brachioli intranei rapiua
no uno ueterrimo cãdelabro æneo lucentiſſimo inaurato, i forma di uaſo per una delphinea anſa. Lequale anſe erano duirepandi, & mordi-
ci delphini a duno nodo, & cũ la cauda deriuauano adunce ſopra la corpulétia dil uaſo attenuãtiſe fina alla cõculata hiatura, cum dui altri nodi
uerſo lo orificio. Il quale alquanto in circulare dilatatione, ſopra il labro
ordinataĩte erano infixi quatro acuati pironi, & nel mediano uno, gli al
tri excedeua cũ il pediculo tra le tibie degli pueruli. Tuta queſta ſcalptura
fundata aſſideua ſopra uno quadrato o phyteo dal pauimento ſurgente,
nudo di liniaĩto excepto nel mediano excalpto, uidi uno maritimo
ouero nauale trophæo, penſai i monuĩto dilla uiǎoria adepta, deuiǎa
la claſſe degli rhodii era uno roſtro, ouero parte dila pra roſtrara, duno ue
terrimo nauigio, Nel mediano dilǫ̃le promineua uno trócho, neli rami
dilǫ̃le iueſtita era una militare toraca, & plo exito brachiale, gli rami ſe ex
tédeuano trũcati di cime, ad uno degli diǎi appenſo era p el canono uno
clypeo, Dalaltro uno inſtruméto nauale, ſotto la torace tranſuerſarii nel
trunco dependeuano una ancora, & uno temone, ſopra la cima dil ſtir-
pe exeũte el collario, una criſtata galea era belliſſime appoſita. Lequale tute coſe nõ e da credere, che ſencia ſymmetria, & maximo artificio fuſſeron
exquiſitamente cum tuti gli requiſiti liniamenti expreſſo, & faberrimaĩ
te depolito, digno di ſpeǎatura & memorato æterno. La comméſuratio-
ne dilquale, chi ſa la proportione dilla ſeſquialtera facilmente il conduce
ra perfeǎo. Suſpicai che da uno gli ſcalptori dil Mauſoleo & queſto fuſſe
abſoluto.

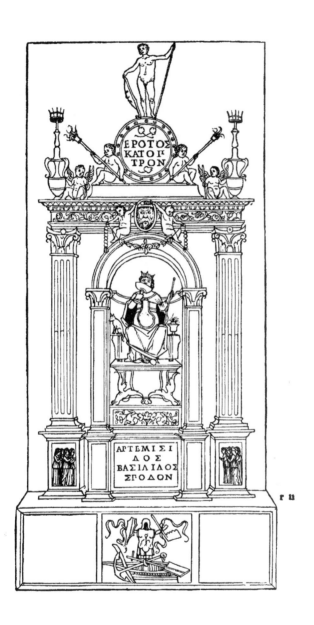

Γ ιι

Facile non mi fe præsta,cum quãta hylaritudine io accuratissimamẽ
te miraua tanto di memorato uenerãde opere opportunaméte narrare.
Cum lanimo piu irritato sempre cofe di nouo ritrouare. Dique alhora
gliochii mei dal magnifico & superexcellente sepulchro apena di
moti,Ancora per le ftrumofe congerie di ruinamenti exquifitamente explorando , trouai etiam uno elegantiffimo
faxo.Nelquale cum incredibile politura, afcalpti mi
rai dui nudi pueruli, una bipartita cortinula rife-
ranti,Vno de qui & laltro deli monftrando
due belliffime tefte,Di adolefcente luna,& di una ingenua uirgine lal
tra,cum uno miferando ca-
fo nel Epitaphio di
perfecte notule
fufcripto
tale.

✳

✳ ✳

✳

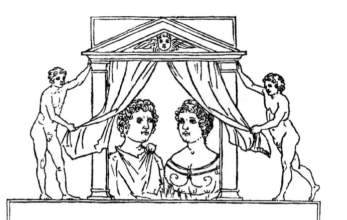

ASPICE VIATOR.Q.SERTVLLII ET DVLCICV
LAE SPON.MEAE.ℭRANCILIAE VIRG.SIMVL
AC.POST INDE QVID FACIAT LICENTIOSA
SORS LEGITO.IN IPSA FLORIDA AETAT.CVM
ACRIOR VIS AMORIS INGRVER.MVTVO CA
PT.TAND.SOCERO.E.ET.M.SOCR.ANNVEN
TIB.SOLENNI HYMEN.NVPT.COPVLAMVR.
SED O FATVM INFOEL.NOCTE PRI.CVM IM
PORT.VOLVPTATIS EX.L.FAC.EXTINGVERE
ET.D.M.V.VOTA COGEREMVR REDD.HEV IP
SO IN ACTV DOM.MARITALIS CORRVENS AM
BIAM EXTRE.CVM DVLCITVDINE LAETISS.
COMPLICATOS OBPRESSIT.FVNESTAS SO
ROR.NEC NOVI QVID FECISS.PVTA. NON E
RAT IN FATIS TVM NOSTRA LONGIOR HO.
RA.CARI PARENTES LVCTV NEC LACHRYMIS
MISERA AC LARVATA NOSTRA DEFLEATIS
FVNER AN EREDDATIS INFOELICIORA
ATVOS NOSTROS DIVTVR
NIORES VIVITE ANNOS
OPTIME LECTOR
AC VIVE TVOS.

r iij

Non molto diftante da quefto,alquanto commoto a fufpiruli p il pcedendente i fœlice cafo lecto,trouai uno altro fpectando &digniffimo monumento,cum due ftriate colúnelle una per lato,femicycle exacte dal folido
faxo,marmoro candidiffimo,cú bafule&capitelli,trabecula,zophorulo
coronicule,&faftigiolo,nella figura triquetra,dilquale due albicante tur
turule i uno uafculo cóbibeuano.Nel contento tra le ftriate di curto infcalpto era uno inarcuato fuffito, æquaméte diftributo i quadriculi lacu
nulati,ouero per fingulo occupaua una pentaphila a norma optica ,minuentifi le liniature cum il contento.Sotto ilquale una artificiofa arca alquanto promineua,appacta cú due porticule.In una dillequale itrauano
imagine nude.Nellaltra puelli nudi uffiuano, cú gli tituli nel mediano cótenti,coniecturai ragioneuolmente indicare quefto mondo
effere una arca ,cum due porte,chi entra morédo,&chi ne effe
nafcendo,& uno &laltro plorabondi , laquale iaceua fopra
dui harpyiatici piedi in folliatura conuerfi,& nel medio uno pede puro di liniamento.Soto la ligatu
ra dil curto uoltato.tale epitaphio mirai
di i pietofo & difperato cafo .
Nel refiduo tali infigni uidi.

*

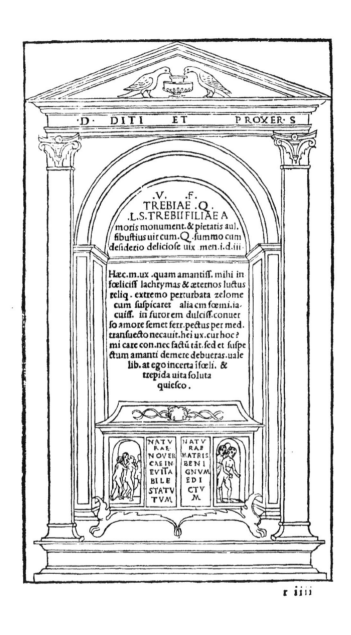

VIII. ALDUS' LATER YEARS

ALDUS WAS KNOWN AND ESTEEMED AMONG the elite collectors and intellectuals of Europe. His press and the academy of Greek scholars, which he founded in order to facilitate the printing of the Greek classics, was a paradigm of turbulent, driven, idealistic Renaissance Europe. Sometime between the appearance of St. Catherine's *Epistole* and the precedent-breaking Virgil, Aldus founded his Neaccademia — a new academy in direct descent from Plato's original one — with scholars and literary men who were to be for him what the editorial director and his staff of editors is for a publishing house today. More and more, as his editions grew, did Aldus feel the need both of help in his arduous task and also of diverse learned opinion concerning texts. His own friends and acquaintances informally provided the scholarly resources he had been using.

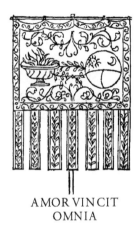

AMOR VINCIT
OMNIA

Now he found that the most convenient and efficient way to procure their advice was to form them into a body meeting regularly and known variously as the Neaccademia, Philhellenist Academy, or more popularly, the Aldine academy. It was the fifth in Italy, following the two in Rome – which Aldus would have heard of in his student days – Cosimo de' Medici's Neo-Platonic academy in Florence and the Neapolitan academy. Aldus' academy was emphatically Greek in inspiration and resembled that of Cardinal Bessarion in Rome not only in its purpose but also because of its personal style – the members met in the home of the founder, and the academy lasted only the founder's lifetime. In Aldus' preface to the 1502 Sophocles, there is an intimate glimpse of academy members sitting around the fire discussing textual preparation of the next endeavor.

Perhaps the academy was already prenoted in Aldus' occasional reference to his first working residence at Sant' Agostino as "thermae." Four times in the course of his career does Aldus refer to his shop by that term. His first catalog of October 1, 1498 is issued *in thermis Aldi Romani*. Perhaps he is indicating, by his use of the word for a public establishment in antiquity where one could bathe and, by extension, meet people for conversation or social gatherings, that his shop is also such a meeting place. The new academicians were expected to speak Greek at all meetings, and the fines levied against the delinquents were to accumulate until there was a significant amount,

WHICH SUM WOULD BE "CONSIGNED TO SI-
GNOR ALDO SO THAT HE HAS THE MEANS
WHEREBY TO INVITE US *SPLENDIDAMENTE* TO
A BANQUET, NOT IN THE USUAL MANNER OF
PRINTERS, BUT AS BEFITS THOSE WHO DREAM-
ING OF THE NEW ACADEMY, INSTITUTED IT
IN THE MANNER OF PLATO."[55]

n this practical arrangement of a consultive board of experts, each of whom would edit in his particular field, Aldus once again showed a fine perception of the editorial role in publishing. The disorder of publications at that time showed keenly the need for direction. It is presumable that another function of the academy members was to provide texts for Aldus, or search them out for him on any journeys they made. In the preface to his 1508 Pliny Aldus says that his edition owes its importance to the use of a manuscript ("most correct and of a marvelous and venerable antiquity") found some years earlier in Paris by Fra Giocondo of Verona and known as the Parisinus manuscript.

For a time Aldine editions were published in the name of the academy with colophons reading *ex Academia nostra* or *in Academia Aldi*. However, by 1505 the affairs of the academy seemed in disarray, and one of the members writing to another noted that Aldus was better from his recent illness, but it was the academy that was failing.[56] Among the academy members were Fra Giocondo, Andrea d'Asola, Alberto Pio, Pietro Bembo, Marcus Masurus, and Marin Sanudo, all of whom figured so intimately in Aldus' life. There were also more distant members like Erasmus of Rotterdam and Thomas Linacre of

Canterbury. Erasmus corresponded with Aldus and came to dwell with him in Venice while Aldus prepared Erasmus' work for press. And in the preface to his *Adages* Erasmus compared the glory of Aldus to that which Ptolemy gained in creating the great library at Alexandria. But, Erasmus wrote, whereas the library of Ptolemy "was contained between the narrow walls of its own house," Aldus was "building up a library which has no other limits than the world itself."[57]

* *

*

ERASMUS was almost forty when he arrived in Italy in 1506. There he went first to Turin and then to Bologna where he met a collaborator of Aldus. It is from Bologna that Erasmus writes to Aldus, offering his translations of Euripides, for he was discontent with a previous edition because of the many errors. "I would consider my labors assured of immortality," he wrote to Aldus, "if they were given to the light from your press, especially in those small characters that are more beautiful than any others."[58]

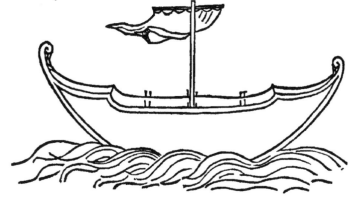

Aldus accepted and invited Erasmus to Venice where they discussed the text, and the *Hecuba* and *Iphigenia in Aulis* were rapidly issued in italic in December 1507, the only book published that year. The previous year Aldus' press had been completely inactive as the consequence of his absence from Venice.

This first communication between the two humanists, Aldus and Erasmus, had been an invitation on Aldus' part for Erasmus to visit the academy. When Erasmus lived and worked with Aldus, preparing the compilation of proverbs and sayings from antiquity called the *Adages* that Aldus would publish in 1508, his addition to the household brought the total to thirty-three. In addition to the family members — the family consisting of both Aldus' and Andrea's households — there were the permanent guests and academy members like Scipione Fortiguerra and Girolamo Aleandro, the servants, and those who worked with the press and had meals provided as part of their wages. Erasmus, in his *Opulentia sordida*, written many years after the death of his colleague Aldus, would comment caustically on the meagerness of the meals provided in the household of the affluent but parsimonious Andrea Torresani and his hapless son-in-law Aldus.

* * * *
* * *
* *
*

Erasmus, speaking Latin, joined the work crew in the shop and, as recorded in his correspondence,[59] read and selected from the codices and wrote his commentary amid the clatter of the presses so that Aldus could print the pages with great dispatch fresh from the hands of the author. The following day typographical errors were corrected and Erasmus would read the whole proof and make his further corrections. Finally Aldus took over the whole thing. They seemed to have composed the *Adages* at the speed of three pages a day, with the entire work taking eight to nine months. The work was published in 1508 with

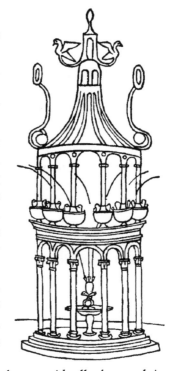

Aldus stating in the preface that he put aside all other work in order to publish such a learned and useful book.

Erasmus finally left Italy for England where he composed *The Praise of Folly*. Here there is an affectionate mention of Aldus who had offered to publish this new work but who died before seeing it when it was published in 1515.

* *
*

FROM 1508 Aldus' life and work are much under the sway of the external factors combining to beleaguer Venice. All the great powers were against her. The resentment against the power and opulence of the Serene Republic grew always greater until a coalition of foreign powers, the League of Cambrai, was formed to wrest Venice's land holdings in the Veneto and divide them among France, the Empire, Spain and the pope, who had excommunicated Venice.

Hostilities began in 1509. It is curious to note that in the conspiracies of foreign nations that dragged Venice to the brink of ruin, Alberto Pio, the student and benefactor of Aldus, was one who helped prepare the scenario of war and disaster in his role as an ambassador who reconciled France with the Empire against Venice. His dominion over Carpi had been lost, regained, then finally lost, and he spent his last years in Paris completely dispossessed of his lands. All this influenced the Aldine press, which had suspended activity in 1506-7, except for the *Euripides* of Erasmus, but was starting up with renewed vigor in 1508. However, following Pope Julian II's edict against Venice that stipulated that all who were in trade there were enjoined to leave, conditions were such in the Republic in 1509 that Aldus sought refuge for himself and his family in Ferrara, hoping for the protection of Lucrezia Borgia, the duchess of Ferrara, to whom he had dedicated his publication of the poems of Ercole Strozzi. With the exigencies of the time, Aldus and Andrea dissolved the pooling of their goods. Both lost, then eventually recovered, their properties

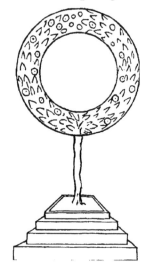

in the Venetian *terra firma*. And in this period Aldus' family grows: three sons are born and two daughters, of whom the younger will die in childhood.

* *
*

YET WITH ALL this turmoil and these trials, Aldus is once again in Venice by July 1512 to take up his work in the last phase of his career, with thoughts of resuscitating his academy as he writes to Lucrezia Borgia and offers her the possibility of acquiring another merit in her crown of good deeds by helping to support the academy.

When Aldus took up his work again, he was even contemplating printing books in Hebrew. He had only the Crysolaras grammar ready for press, the only book he managed to publish in 1511, in addition to a third edition of the Lascaris grammar. He succeeded, however, in 1513 to cap his endeavors by publishing three works very close to his heart: the Greek orators, the works of Pindar, and the works of Plato in a folio edition. With the appearance of Plato's works, the great task of Aldus was completed: all the major works of classical Greek literature had been brought into print. Thanks to Aldus' zeal in unearthing manuscripts and making them accessible, very little remained unpublished or unknown from antiquity. After Aldus' time only two tragedies of Euripides and a play by Menander would come to light. The fundamental monument to Greek glory was published in Aldine editions.

Aldus dedicated his Plato to the Medici pope, Leo X, son of Lorenzo the Magnificent and a great Renaissance patron who said at his elevation in 1513, "Since God has given us the papacy, let us enjoy it." In his long preface to the pope, Aldus speaks of his aspirations and toil and says, "I go on like Sisyphus rolling my boulder without being able to get it to the top of the mountain: the learned, it's true, from every part of the world love me for my labors and compare me to Hercules for not succumbing under the weight of such hard enterprises...." Nonetheless, he says, "up to now I have not published a single book that has satisfied me, and my love for letters warns me that there hasn't yet issued from my press into the hands of the studious a single book that was as correct as I would have desired. So much so, that when, through my distraction or that of other correctors, there escapes us any error, however small, I feel such displeasure that I'd give, if I could, a ducat for each to correct them...."[60]

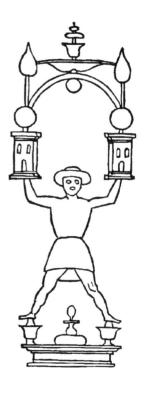

*   *   *

*

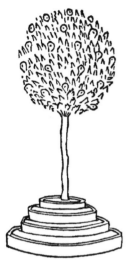

By this time his team of collaborators had suffered attrition, and few
friends remained to count on, but among
them the steadfast Masurus, Egnazio,
and Andrea Navagero. Because of the
eminence of their personal situations
these three men must not have weighed
heavily on the budget of the press. Masurus was a public professor, Egnazio
the prior of St. Mark's, and Navagero
a young Venetian at the beginning of
an illustrious career as historian and
ambassador of the Serene Republic.

The last editions of Aldus' career
are a miscellanea: among others, Fra Giocondo's commentary
on Caesar's commentaries, which initiates a new kind of book;
a reprint of Cicero's letters; the Latin writings on agronomy;
Suetonius; and Quintilian. As Aldus mentions in his preface
to Cicero's *De arte rhetorica,* dedicated to Andrea Navagero,
he is still hindered in his studies and work by "first of all, the
numerous letters of learned men which are sent to me from
all over.... I either reply not at all when the letter is not very
interesting, or, if it is important, I answer very briefly.... Then
there are those who visit me, some to greet me, some to find out
what is new, and...the largest number for lack of anything
else to do – they say, 'Let's go to see Aldus.' They come in
droves and sit around idly.... I have taken care to warn them,
by putting up a notice, like an edict, on the door of my office,
to this effect: 'Talk of nothing but business, and despatch that
business quickly.'"[61]

ALDUS WAS NOT technically a typesetter; he not only never composed a line of type himself, but it was his weakness not to see the exigencies of typeface to be clarity and legibility over his penchant for imitative hand-writing. The case of his Greek type shows him at his weakest. "His Greek letters by every standard are about as bad as they well could be, his romans vary from mediocrity to supreme excellence, while his italics turned out to be one of the most successful innovations of typographical history."[62]

Since Greek printing was his chief personal concern, he bears responsibility for the disastrous consequences of his decisions in the cutting of Greek typefaces. At the moment when Aldus entered publishing history, very little was available in printed form except school texts. In 1490, when Aldus set up his press, only Homer, Theocritus and Isocrates had been printed. In those texts, as well as in the grammars and other school books, the Greek type had been designed by printers who imitated simple letter forms culled from manuscripts and coin inscriptions.

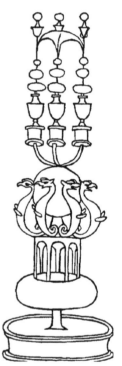

Aldus, however, did not have typographical criteria as his top priority.
Aldus' approach was of a scholar thoroughly imbued in Greek, even in the writing of it.

* *

He was accustomed to the use of numerous abbreviations and ligatures,
which could economize a writer's time
and paper. This economy, however,
was offset by making type-casting and
composition vastly more difficult for
typesetters trying to duplicate hand-
written letters that are connected. Still,
Aldus adopted a Greek font containing no less than 462 sorts, including
abbreviations, so that the editions of
the Greek classics in which he took
such pride became for later scholars
almost undecipherable unless they
mastered that kind of shorthand.

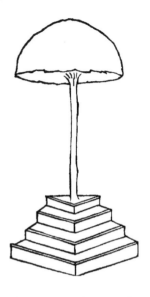

Aldus' distinction is as a scholar-publisher, the director of a
great publishing house. Always non-complacent of his achievements, he continued right up to his death to entertain plans for a
polyglot Bible to be printed in Hebrew, Greek, and Latin. "What
he did achieve was to raise the prestige of the mass-produced book
by convincing a more exclusive market that it was reputable...."[63]
He was a man of vision and ideals who, in his prefaces, advocated
the improvement of society through education. Aldus established
his eminence presenting critical editions based on the best procur-
able sources. His sensibility into the true value of the press was
as an instrument of civilization. The concepts that guided his
editorial work have dominated modern editorial practice among
those publishing houses that hold to high standards.

Curt Buhler, a noted commentator on Aldine editions,
gives this summary: of the 132 books that Aldus published in

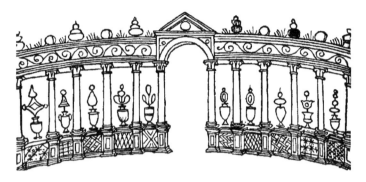

twenty years of activity, there were seventy-three classics (thirty-four in Latin, thirty-nine in Greek), eight in vernacular Italian, twenty contemporary works in Latin, and eighteen school-books, of which twelve were in Greek. Of forty-nine *editiones principes* of Greek works among all publishers, Aldus alone accounted for thirty. His printing activity was intense except for the war period of 1506-12 when he produced altogether only eleven books. In other years, however, he averaged better than eleven books per year.[64]

* *
*

ALDUS' BOOKS were truly his monument, and when he died on February 8, 1515, his fellow academician and friend, the patrician diarist, Marin Sanudo, records the impressive scene of Aldus, "excellent humanist and Hellenist," laid in state in the church of San Paternian, his bier surrounded by copies of all the books from his press. He died with his reputation for honesty, modesty, and faithfulness in his endeavors completely intact.

Matteo Bandello (1485-1561), famous for his *Novelle* – short tales, including one of Romeo and Juliet, a reputed source of Shakespeare's play, which once interested Aldus who had read a few and was considering their publication, mentioned the loss of the great publisher in a dedicatory letter: "The most learned man, Aldo Manuzio, worthy to have lived many centuries, died without ever having been praised fully enough...."[65]

It was said of Brunelleschi that when constructing the
cupola of the Duomo in Florence he was so exacting
that not one single brick was put in place that he
had not first approved by hand and eye to be
sure it was without defect. He was building
not for himself, but for the centuries.
And so with Aldus: no book left his
press that he had not overseen.
He, too, in his zeal to
popularize learning,
created for the
centuries.[66]

* * * *

* * *

* *

*

decorati,di parua & mediocre ftatura,& uarie auicule & ucelleti de qui ,&
de li inftabilmēte uolitando puaganti,mo fu,mo giu cū delectabile garito
faltanti la fuaue fonoritate dil fuo canto per tuto rifonante.Ilquale uirtute hauuto harebbe qualūque filuicola & inepto core a piacere,gaudio , &
folacio di prouocare,feftigianti cum le fue alete & plumule.Quiui la q̄-
rulante lufcinia Dedalione la morte dilla filiola di Licaone piāgente ,gli
maculati meruli,& la cantante Corydalo,ouero galerita ,& la terrancola,
parco ,ouero alauda.Gli folitarii pafferi.Pfitaco eloquentiffimo,di multi
plice ueftito,uiride bianco,luteo,phœniceo ,& giallo cum uerde.La uni-
ca(ma non quiui)& marauegliofa phœnice,a canti candidiffime turture.
Pico marito di Pomona,le tumide iracondie di Cyrce manifeftante.Ido
na dil dilecto marito Ithilo lachrymofa.Aftarie cum gli calciati piedi di
rofato.Et le due piche, Progne Tectacola.Et la pia Antigone troppo bel
la fencia lingua.Itys dolorofa & funefta menfa . Il gulatone Icteris.
Tereo faxicola in le piume le regie pompe feruante,qu æritabondo
ⲧⲩ̄ⲙⲩ̄,pu,pu,nel canto fuo,& nel capo gerulo & infignito dil
la militare crifta, & da Syringa il foporato paftore .Et gli u-
célli di Palamede, Et que querdula, & la lafciua Perdice
Et Porphyrio.Periclimeno la cui forma Iupiter li-
centemente ad gli fui amori hae ufato. Et la Sy-
golida ,ouero Melancorypho,ouero Atri
capilla . Nellautūno mutabile. Similmente Erythaco,ouero Phenicu-
ro,& altri innumeri di pro-
lixo narrato.
✳✳✳
✳

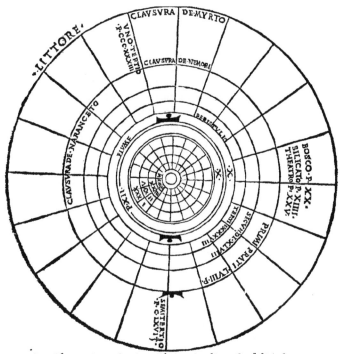

Per piu euidente dimonſtratione, Il circuito di queſta delitioſa & amœ-
niſſima inſula di circúmenſuratione conſtaua di tre milliarii. La figura
dillaquale di uno milliario il ſuo diametro præſtaua. Ilquale in diuiſione
tripartito, uno tertio. 333. paſſi continiua uno pede, & dui palmi, & alquã
to piu dalextremo labro dille litorale ripe fina al clauſtro naranceo. La
menſura di uno ſemitertio, paſſi. 166. & palmi. 10. occupaua. Daqueſto ter
mine icominciauano gli prati uerſo il centro tendenti, altro tanto ſemitertio. Diſtributo dúque acconciamente uno integro tertio, rimane uno
ſemitertio a diſpenſare fina al meditulo, paſſi. 166. & palmi, io. Dal periſty
lio antedicto, era conceduto alquanto di ſpatio rimaſto per la contractio
ne degli prati ſopradicti, ad euitare lãguſtia dille quadrature. Gliquali
non haueuano il ſuo termine fina al cópimto dil tertio, et queſto ſolertem
te aduene p proportionare alquáto il qdrato ultimo p le linee al púcto di
ducte. Ilquale ſpatio tra il flume & il periſtylio intercalato, tuto gratioſa-

Da quefto fpectatiffimo colūnato fina ad gli fequenti gradi,era com
planato i una marmoraria ftrata circūgyrante,in latitudine pedi feni.
Oue imediate incōminciauano altri feptem gradi a falire , cum la p̄ fata
opatura,menfuratione,& materia,& colorameto,& tuto quefto negli fe
quenti era riferuato integramente.
Sopra il fupremo era una capfea excauatura,pedi quatro in aptione.
Il patore dillaqualea fufficientia era profundo, & cufi negli fequenti.
nellaquale nafceua uno fepto buxeo , quale uitrina illuftratione gratiffi
mamente uirente. Et allibella degli ponti,& ftrate,mirai una turre dilla
dicta uirentia , fubleuata pedi noue,& lata cinque,cum una patéte por
ta inhiato pedi tre,& alta fei,& cufi le fequente.
Quefto primo fepto di craffitudine tripedale,& di fei alto , & cufi gli
fequenti,uedeuafi di foliamento denfiffimo, & era cufi difpofito di pin
natura dilla propria arboratione.Tra una & laltra turre uidi egregiamē
te facto uno triumpho cum caballi,una rheda trahéti,& p̄cedenti lo o-
uante alcuni militi macherophori,& cum hafte triumphale artificiofa-
mente compacti uariando belliffime leopere. In uno altro interturrio
promineua una nauale enyo.Tra due altre turre clafica pugna terreftre.
Tra due altre uenatione & antiquarie fabule damore.Cum diligentiffi-
mo expreffo,& exquifitiffima deformatione.Tale ordine circūueniēn-
te uariando le fequentie.
Intro quefto primario circuuallato,dapo una ambiente ftrata ,qua-
le quella inferiore tra il columnulato,& gli gradi di mirabile teffellatu-
ra offeriuafe di grande admiratione,& exceffiuamente delectabile artifi
cio,fencia dubio di fatichare omni humana intuitione & fenfo.Ilqua-
le nel primo afpecto tapeti charaini difpofiti & extenfi ftratamente alla
planitie,facilmente arbitrai,Cum tute maniere di coloratione , che a ta
le oftentatione meritamente expediua exprimere , in modo di gratiofa
picturatione conducta in piu uariate & multiplice ingrupature & figu
re & figni cum la opportuna diuerfitate di coloramenti,di holufcule al
la requifita diftinctione dilla opera ficta. Alcune plene di colore, Altre
cum obfcura coloratione,Alcune mediocremente,tale piu chiare & fe
ftichine,alcune prafine,altre di uirore palide,alcune meno, & di fubru
bicundo coloramento,cum iucundiffima conciliatione. Le figure prí
cipale continente in fe multiplice defignature, era tra due rhóbee, una
circulare,& una rhomboida tra dui circuli, alternantife continuamēte
in gyro,exempta quella parte,oue le uie intercallauano prouidamente
relicte.Lequale ftrate fempre tra due uniforme figuratione paffauano.
                                                                    Lequale

Lequale deformatione extauano infepte in uno circulare liniaméto imitante(come e dicto)la figura ifularia. Et primo erano circúdate dalla ftrata ambiente,p xima al buxeo clauftro,colligata emuficataméte cum le recte tédente al centro. Lequale ftrate erano filicate,la mediana parte,di fe pte partitióe ,tre aquiftaua per fe ,di nigerrima petra dura & fpeculare,che di cufi facta nigritudine coticula indice nel flume ocho non fatrouereb be,& de qui,& de li coniuncte immediate erano una partitione di petra la ctea,di tale albentia,quale nó fe uide il compofito lacticinio murianenfe contumaciffima & plucida,gli extremi erano due altre portione, una de qui & laltra de li di finiffima petra rubentiffima piu che ftriffo corallio,& intra la nigra erano impacte faberrimamente le tefellature. Quefta uenu, fta difpofitione obferuata fe continia per tute le fequente, degli fequenti clauftri.

Tra le recenfuite ftrate interfticiamente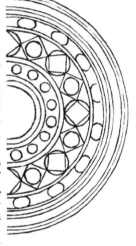
circúfepte erano le pfcripte figure. Détro
le rhóboide,circuli. Détro gli circuli gli
rhóbi. Dapofcia uarie figure implicite di
fœcúdiffimo & gratiofo cogitato. Nellóbilico dille rotúde,plantato fe attolleua u
no alto cupffo. Nel meditullo degli rhóbi uno dritiffimo & comofo pino. Simil
mente negli circinanti frigii intra gli limi
ti dille ftrate,di uno & laltro extremo, cú
il moderato diftributo di uarie opature,
& figure ouolate ,& hemiale, nel puncto
mediano infurgeuano uerdiffime urathe,
per lo intermediato cuprefeo & pineo cor
refponfiue,& cum il cacuminato æquale,
& dilla granditudine uniforme.Degli rami folte & di ordine cuprefino,ufate dalla
diuina matre a cœlare la calumnia.Dapo
fcia agli conuenienti lochi folertemente
gli fpectatiffimi fiori erano communicati di qualúcha coloratione difpé fata,cum harmonia elegantiffime cú redolente fragrantia.

Di uno & laltro fexo in quefti belliffimi & amœniffimi uireti interual lati incollauano effi folaméte allo pera dilla fœtofa natura dediti, & al cul to contenti adcóferuatione di tale opere olitare operantife. Ne tanta dili gentia il iuftiffimo Re di Pheaci Alcinoo monftroe circa la cuftodia de gli fui horti olitorii,quanta quiui era obferuata, cum mirifico , & fedulo

u iii

ſtudio omni coſa applicata gemella, nel loco ſuo deſtinato innata apparé
do. Colluſtrata degli marmori cum diſtincto ſplendore, & cuſi le circina
ture ſequente.

IL SEC VNDO clauſtro olitorio ſequita immediate dapo la proxi,
ma recitata operatura. Nel extremo dillaquale ordinataméte gli altri ſep,
teni gradi uerſo il centro incohauano. Sopra lultimo era compacta u,
na uariata concluſura di arborario coloramento ſummamente ſpectatiſ,
ſima, cum turre, ouero ſpecule optimamente congeſte di Narancii, &
collateraneamente alla porta erano in ordine implantati dui ſtipiti, cioe
tra il pariete dilla turre, & tra la pertione, ouero alamenti dilla porta, que,
gli fora dil culmo dilla turre extollentiſe, mutuamente ſe colligauano in
uno redacti, ſublati dal ſupremo dilla turre tripedali. Poſcia la ſulta fron,
datione principiaua deformantiſe in uno moderato cupreſſo. Et cuſi in
circuito per tutte, di dui paſſi la ſua procericate. Lo interturrio ſepto di co
loramento uariaua, & di arboramento, tra due era texuto di iunipero. Tra
dualtre di lentiſco. Poſcia di comari, di Liguſtro. Di Dendro Liuano, Di
Cynocanthe. Di Olea. Di Lauro. Cum uno modo ſempre nel ſuo recen
te uirore frondeo. Reiterádo dopo lultimo il primario ſucceſſiuamente
belliſſime di opera topiaria, immune di oſtentatione ſtipea, cum non pe,
riture fronde.

Oue tra due turre ſopra il planato, in medio uno mirando pinnato e,
mineua Imperoche interſtitiamente dil murale ſepto, profiliuano pian,
te di buxo, cum exquiſito artificio conducti in ſymmetriate lune corni,
cularie, acompimento dil ſpatio interturrio, cum il ſuo patore, ouero hia
to ſupinato, cú ſingulare diligentia deformate. Nel mediano tra dui cor,
ni ſaliua uno iunipero gradatamente decado pinato, fina alla cima atte,
nuátiſi, quale ſi al torno turbinate fuſſeron, & coæquate le pungente fró
dule. La piu craſſa nel mediano hiato collocata. Tra il cornicio aſcende,
ua ſurrecto uno ſtipite tráſcendendo uno pedi & ſemiſſe, Oue rotunda,
ua una pila buxea iuſtiſſimamente pportionata.

Intro queſto clauſtramento, tra gli limiti dille uie erano quadrati ho,
luſcularii di miráda factura, diſſimili di diſignatione olearia alternabon
do acópimento di tutto queſto ſpectando circuito.

Il primo quadrangulo per le ſtrate dalaltro diſcriminato, per lequale
illegitimi quadri euadeuano, era una inodatura dil liniamento quadrale
per faſcicule deformato, cú maxima politura, late palmi tre. La prima fa
ſcia nel mediano era in circulo demigrata, & dagli dui anguli ſe ricontra,
uano le faſcie al circinare, luna ſupna dillaltra. Il quale annulo in ſe unal,
tra faſcia inodaua, diuiſi dalla prima incluſiue pedi quatro. Et quella par
te dil

te dil circulo,che era fuperiore ,fubigeua allaltra fafcia,& cufi mo lũa,mo laltra alternantife inferna & fuperna.Et q̃fta quadratura fecunda , nel fuo angulo fe inannulaua occupando da angulo ad angulo femp̃ alternatam̃ te feruãdo lo liniamento fafciale , mo fupernate,mo infernate,alla regula tione degli nodi.

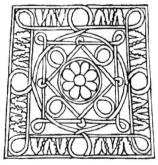

Gli primi ãnuli fe ampliauano dẽtro al fecũdo quadrato ,facẽdo una circinãte rotundatione per la capacitate di effo quadrato. Da-pofcia fe caufaua unaltro quadra to æquidiftante dal fecundo,quã to effo fecundo dal primo .et q̃fto fimilm̃te il fuo angulo fe incircu-laua,uerfo langulo dil fecũdo,fo-pra la linea diagonia,intricantife, cum la rotundatione,fcandendo & fubigendo.Dentro quefto no-uiffimo quadrato rhõbeaua una figura.Gli anguli dillaquale cum ftricti uoluti innodulauano il media-no dilla fafcia di l ultimo interno quadrangulo.

Nel fpatio triãgulare tra il rhõbo & lo iterfticio quadrato ,fopra le linee diagonie,ad i plem̃to era uno libero circu lo,Dẽtro il rhõbo era uno circulo p la ca-pacitate dilla figura rhõbea difnodato · In medio dilquale circulo,era una octophyl la rofa.Nel cẽtro dillaq̃le era conftituita u na inane ara,rotũdata di petra di flauo nu midico cũ tre capitale offature di boue,tra luna & laltra di temerario exfcalpto pãda uano fafciculi di fronde & fructi ,nel me-dio turgefcẽti,cũ uagabondi lori circa gli capi ligando innodati,& cingiendo gli fa fciculi,cũ eximio liniam̃to,al focco & al-labaco cũ belliffima fima,& altri ornati de corabõdi.Fora dillaquale ara nafceua una fauina,in forma compacta cu preffina ,fti pata la apertione di lara di multiplici che-rophile.

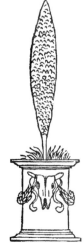

La expreffione olitoria dilla pictura dil pcedente quadrato, cufi era il
coloramento diftributo. Et primo la prima fafcia era denfiffima di fanfu
co. La fecunda di aurotano. La tertia di chamæpiteos. Il rhóbo di ferpil-
lo montano . La rotundatione contenta nel rhóbo di Chamædryos. La
rofa di uiolarii ametheftini. In circuito dilla rofa & fuori dil fuo ambito
erano di uiole olorine, cum le uiole denfiffimamente florei. Gli quatro
circuli intro lultimo quadrato, negli trianguli facti dal rhombo ,& quadrato inclufi erano di mellantio, oueramente Gyth. Intro uiole luteole.
Tutto lo infepto in quefti trianguli di Cyclamio. Gli circuli tra il primo
& fecondo quadrato erano completi di ruta. Gli circuli dil tertio di primula ueriffllorida. Nel primo ambito tra il primo , & il fecúdo quadrato
erano defignate foliature acanthine , una tra due oppofita, erano di polio montano , limitate tra adiantho . Nel centro degli circuli collocati
fopra gli diagonii per ciafcuno era fublato circa uno pede & femiffo una
pila, cum æqua legie in tutti feruata, di altitudine & fphærica craffitudine
& collocatione, exclufi gli quatro caufati dal interfito quadrato negli an
guli diagonali. Negliquali nel centro fe attolleuano tricubitali cauli di
malua rofaria purpurea, & molochinea, plurifolia & pentaphylla, cú lar-
go prouento floreo. Nel fecundo fentonica. Nel fecundo dendroliuano,
Negli deformati dalla figura circulare contenta cum la exteriore & pria-
ria fafcia quadra, nel centro erano pile di Ifopo . Dalle ambiente ftrate &
recte al centro, & tranfuerfarie propinque al uirente fepto , & ppinque a
gli gradi lo exclufo, tanta era la quadratura, & degli reliqui.

Laltro fociale quadrato di quefta conclufura molto periucundo , &
uenufto, & mirabile operatura , & cómeto, & mirifica diftributione olito
ria, & nobiliffima inodatura , di coloramento di uarii fimplici diftincta.
Proximo ad gli marmorarii limiti dille ambiente ftrate nel quadrato, da
quelle interftitio deformato, & relicto circúimitaua una fafcia pedale, &
dodrante. Dallaquale coniugatamente fe partiuano tute le fafcie uniforme ad compofitione dilla operatura di quefto quadrato . Dalaltro per la
interpofita ftrata difcriminato. Erano noue quadri, æquidiftanti, per il ca
pro dil principale quadrato. Gliquali da qualúque angulo ad angulo, lu
no cum laltro fe copulauano, cum fectione mediana, luna cum laltra dil
le fafcie cum iufto obuio, & tale liniamento impleua il quadrato finien-
do & coeunte cum la extrema fafcia . Per laquale defignatione tra quefti
quadri uno octogonio fe caufaua, includentife gli quadri luno cum laltro. Tra gli anguli degli quadri æque formato era unaltro quadro, cú le
pleure uerfo gli dicti anguli conftituto. Sopra ciafcuna obuia fectione , i
demon-

demonstratione rhombea connodato, cum gli sui anguli ancora, & essi, & transuersaria, & perpendiculariamente coniugati, & per tale mutuo có mercio, & similmente questi uno altro octogonio, nel primo intruso bel latulamente formauano, consotialmente gli noue quadri inclaustrádo.

Dique tutte queste figuratione luna cum laltra colli-
gátise, sotto & supra & alter
nantise, una elegante inno
datura di multiplice figura
mento gratiosamente ren-
deuano. Tutto questo qua-
drato completamente figu
rando. Lequale deformatu
re erano liniate, per plastre
nel solo infixe, candidissi-
mo di marmoro, semido-
drante la sua crassitudine
superficiale, & de qui & deli gli simplici circúparietá
do. Intro ilquale lapideo i-
clusio, intra limitate le her
buscule uariatione coæqtis-

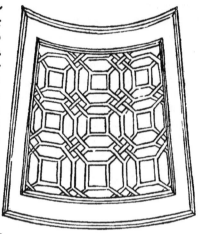

sime & sultamente congerminauano a persecta expressione dil figuramé
to, & questo tuto similmente obseruato per omni tale cóposito artificiosa
mente constaua. Ostentatione, me Iupiter, conspicua, & ad gli sensi sum-
me iucundissima.

Il distributo picturariamente olusculario tale se præstaua, omni inter
clusio libero quadrale cóuestito era di florido Cyclamio. Le fascie sue di
myrsinites. Gli fasciali limiti degli altri inodati cum il sectitio obuio era
herbescente di polio montano. Gli quatro quadriculi dilla incruciata se
ctione, intro il quadro colligato cótecti erano tutti di serpillo. Gli octo-
gonii circumuallando gli liberi quadri, cum requisita sortitione di her-
buscule cusi præstauano uirenti. Vno di Laurentia. Vno di Tarchon. Il
tertio di Achilea. Il quarto di Senniculo. Il quinto di Diosmo. Il sexto
di Terrambula. Il septimo di Baccara. Lo octauo di Amaraco. Il nouissi
mo di Polythricho. Questi dui quadrati recésiti alternatamente in gyro
di questo conclusio spectatissimamente adimpiuano.

Ma p cósumatióe degli pcedéti qdrati resta adire di qsto pxime descripto

nel mediáo q̃dro una porphyritica ara refideua negli águli dillaq̃leuicio
alla coronula apacti ,pmineuano quatro capi ueruecei corniculati li-
maceamente, limatamente exfcalpti.Dagliquali fafciculi incuruefcen-
ti pendeuano cum tutti accefforii dilla rotunda recitati. Sopra laquale ia
ceua uno átiquario uafo amphorale ,cum quatro anfe æquidiuife,di optimo fardonice coniugato belliffime cum il fuo familiare Achate, di mi
ro artificio expreffo.Fora dilquale ufciua uno perpollito buxo,cum la í-
ferna pila,ouero rotundatióe di uno paffo il fuo diametro.Nel culmo dil
laquale erano æqualmente pedali & diftincti quatro ftipiti,Et ciafcuno u
na proportionata pila,fopra ciafcuna uno pauone,cum le code demiffe
refideuano,cum il capo in una platina fopra uno mediano ftipite, exce-
dente le quatro pile,fora la platina afcendeua uno ftipite ancora cú quatro rami. Et ciafcuno fuftentaua una pila. Nel mediano fublato il ftipite
teniua unaltra pila.Sopra laquale nafceua uno circulo ouolato, fpande-
ua dui rami per lato,& uno & laltro haueua una pila,& il fimile nel fuo fu
premo,tale difpofitióe ordinariamte era obferuata in omni uafo,unifor-
me, il loco,il buxo,ara,uafo liniamenti .

DI PROXIMO fequita, & gli altri
fepti gradi. Sopra il fublime circúclude-
ua in modo di parietale muro di uerdiffi
mo myrto,cum le turre,come le altre defi
gnate cum gli cupreffi,& cum tuto il refiduo,cum pinnatura claffica optimamen
té congefto. Intro quefto clauftro fimil-
mente erano quadri dui alternati di figuratione olitoria,cum tale defignatura.Era
no dui quadráguli infafciati cum la fym
metria innodatura, & cum il circulo in-
clufiuo,quale modo il quadrangulo pri
mariamente defcripto. Nellaquale circinatione egregiamente picta uedeuafe u-
na Aquila cum le paffe ale il circinao fpa
tio comprehédéte . In loco dillo achan-
tino foliamento illo erano maiufcule ,&
primo al lato leuo tra le due fafcie,nel fpa
tio dagli circuli exclufo . Nel primo e-

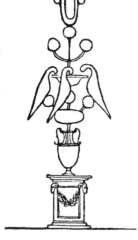

rano due. AL. Nelaltro exclufo quatro.ES.MA.Verfo il fepto,nel primo fpatio tra gli circuli tre .GNA.Et nel fequente quatro.DICA.

Confequentemente uerfo la ftrata, cum il medefimo modo & locatione
quatro. T AOP. Nel altro tre. TIM. Nella extrema uerfo gli gradi, cum
il præfato ordine, & al fcri-
uere feruato, due. IO. Nel
propinquo due. VI.

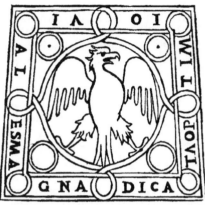

Le fafcie. circuli, & la ro
tundatione interftitia diru
ta denfatamente preffa. La
Aquila di ferpilo. Lo ex-
clufo dagli circuntermini
di polio montano. Le litere di maiorana circůualla-
te di Iua. La cópletione de
gli circuli era di uno, di flo
rante Ianthine, uno di luteole. Il tertio di candide
cum grande fœtura degli
fui flofculi, nunque cadiui, ma perhennemente floribondi. Et le olufcu-
le continuamente cum æquamento uniforme uirente. Interdiĉte proce
dere al deftino dilla fœconda natura. Dal trigonio caufato dalla rotunda
tione, & dagli anguli dille interiore fafcie, era per ciafcuno, uno circulato
dil coloramento herbacio degli concludenti, lo exclufo di Myrfinites.
Nel centro degliquali erano plantate quatro fphærice pile di cópreffif-
fimo myrto, & æquatiffimo, cum bipedale ftipite, & degli reliqui.

Laltro quadrangulo. fafcie. circulo, quale hora e recenfito. Nel circi
nao erano dui uolucri. Daluna parte, una Aquila, & dalaltra obuio uno
Fafiano, cum il roftro direĉto al roftro. Sopra gli labii duno uafo peda-
uano. Ilquale hauea uno pauculo di pediculo, & dal dorfo le ale dambi
due leuate. Tra gli uoluti dille fafcie dalla parte dillaquila nel primo &
inferiore fpatio erano formate tre litere. S VP. Nel altro tre. ER N. Nella
parte fupma nel primo fpatio tre. AE. A. Nel fequente tre. LIT. Dal lato
dil fafiano nel fupernate fpatio tre. I S.B. Nel fubieĉto tre. ENI. Tra le
due infime fafcie nel primo fpatio tre. GNI. Nel fequente tre. T A S.

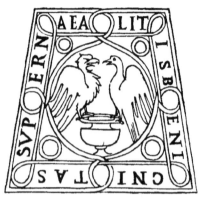

Intro il circuito intrinſe-
camente extra gli conter,
mini dille figuratione, tuto era di polio montano, il
faſciano di laurentia. La a-
quila di fenniculo. Il uaſo
di aſſaro. Nello hiato tra
gli ambienti labii di myrſi
nites. Le extrinſece faſcie-
cú tuto il ſuo corſo di uí-
caperiúca. Laltra faſcia di
trinita. Gli circuli negli á-
guli ítruſi di amaraco. Lo
excluſo & intruſo deglią̃li
di digitello. Le litere di ſerpillo, gli ſpatii di politrico. Gli campi degli ro
tundi faſciali di ſantonica. Negli centri degli circuli tra gli trigoni era u-
na pila, due di olente aurotano, & due di lauendula, ſublata uno pede &
ſemiſſe, ſopra il ſuo ſtipite, negli reliqui alternatamente una pila di ſauina
& una di iunipero tripedale. Tutte le herbe cum uenuſtiſſima foltura, &
freſchiſſimo uirore, & iucundiſſimo perſpecto. Opera miranda di exq-
ſito, di amœnitate, & oblectamento. Irrigate danguſtiſſime fiſtulette ordinatamente diſtribute, uomabonde tenuiſſima & gutticulata aſpergine.
    SEQVENTEMENTE cú ſeruata regula aſcendeuano & altri ſepte-
gradi, ſopra il ſupmo degliquali, una ſpectatiſſima cácellatura circúdaua
tuta di rubente & illuſtriſſimo diaſpide, cú elegáte puiatura, cócordemte-
ad gratiſſime formule cóueniédo, di craſſitudine ſextante. Queſto cacel-
lato ſepto, & il ſequéte era ſencia aptura alcuna, ma continuo, Et quiui fi-
niuano le ſtrate recte al centro inſulano tendente, ma ſolamente conſtaua
uiabile nella ſtrata triumphale, & cuſi il ſequente.
    In queſto uoluptuoſo clauſtro mirai uno nemore di denſitate conſpi-
cuamente ombroſo, di celeberrimo arbuſto. Quiui erano gli dui terebin
thi fœmine, alla uetuſtate pertinace di eximio & nigello ſplédore, di odo-
re iucúdo, bedellio cú roboracea foliatura, malo, ouero medica phéne po
miſera. Hebeno ptioſo, arbore Pipea. Cariophyle. Nuce myriſtica. Il tri-
plice Sandalo. Cinamo. Il laudatiſſimo Silphío, quale nó ſa ritrouerebbe
in la ualle Hiericontha, ouero í Aegypto alla Meterea. Quiui i cádicáte
coſto, quale nó pduce Patale iſula. Et il frutice nardo, cú gli cacumini ia
riſtati, & di ſpica & dil ſuo folio laudatiſſima. Et il xilo aloe di ſuauitate in
enarrabile, q̃lenó deporta lo acephalo Nilo, & il Styrace, & ſtacte. Et
                                                          larbore

l arbore thurea,& myrthea,quale non germina in Sabea,& infiniti altri ar
busculi,& frutici aromatici,cú æquatissimo solo,contecto undique di as
saro,quale non e in púto,ne in Phrygia ,ne i Illirico,emulante il nardo.
Il quale delitiosissimo loco era statione & conuento degli piu noui ,& bel
lissimi ucelleti,che unque ad gli ochii humái fusseron obiecti,uisi, ne co
gniti,alla opera dil amore intenti,subitarii cú gratissimo garulato , tra la
modesta densitate degli rami dilla uiuacissima,& núque cadiua uirétia ca
nore. Il qle beato,& fœlice,pameno & fródoso nemore,le prúpéte aquule
p canaletti & cursiui riuuli dagli liquidi chiarissimi,& sacri fóti,cú sopo-
roso murmure discorreuano.Et quiui sotto le fresche& cóserte umbricu
le,& al suaue reflexo tra le nouelle fróduscule,il multiplice &arguto gari
to discorrédo,inumere & illustre nymphe cú laltro sexo erano latitante,
ad uno discreto piacere da gli altri,& cátáte cum antiquarii instrumti dal
suaue Cupidine fugitiue, & alle opacissime ombre & rurestri facti itente.
Vestiuano deformemte di sericei habiti sutilli &crispuli &cataclisti, di se
microcea tinctura,& la magiore turbula di olorini,& caltuli &galbani,&
alcune di colore colossino,cú crepidule&nymphei calciamini.

Hora tutte le iquiline di questi uoluptuosi lochi ,sentendo il triumpho
so aduento dil sagittáte signore,sencia mora subite obuio festiuante uene
rabóde sapresentorono,le nouissime excepte.Daposcia al suo peculiare
solatio & continuo oblectamento ritornorono.

Postremamte ultra il memorato nemorulo,sencia alcuno itercalato ,&
laltra nouissima gradatióe di septe scalini sequéte,cú obseruata norma ha
ueua sopra il sublime grado una spectatissima cóclusura di uno colúnu-
lato,quale il primo dopo lo antedicto fluuio di artificio & materia.Et q-
ui era circúuallato una sectiliata spatiosa,& expedita,&cóplanata area,cú
mirifico inuéto di tessellato emblematico,& cum inodature di circuleti,
triquetri,quadruli,& conoide figure,& almoide,& hemiale , & rhóboide
& scaline deformato pulcherrime in multiplice designature coeúte,& cú
speculare collustratione,&cum egregio distincto di uaria & eximia colo
ratione.

Finalmente il medio tercio dil milliare,dal flume al cétro i tale cómésio
ne era emusicatamte distributo.Il quale semitertio dúque cóstaua di passi
(como pdicto e) .clxvi . & semisso.Dique al fluuio dati sono passi. xii. al
prato ultra il flume.x.Tuti gli gradi occupauano lógitrorso passi.viii.&
pedi.ii.& i altitudine uniuersale altrotáto.La stratella pedi.vi.Il prio giar-
dino passi.xxxiii.Il secódo.xxvii.Il tercio.xxiii.Il bosco.xxv.La area am
biente il theatro.xvi.Il theatro mediato fina al centro passi .xvi.contini-
ua.Dilla commensuratione insulare ,satis.

VSCITIFORADILLA NAVICVLA ALLINCONTRO
INFINITE NYMPHE VENERONCVMTROPHAEISV
PERBAMENTEINDVTE.POLIPHILONARRA, ET IL
MYSTERIOSOMODO,CHEGLIDIVINI GESTAMÌNI
A CVPIDINE ELLEOFFERIRONO, ETCVM QVALE
HONORARIOPROCESSO,POSTOSEA SEDERE SO-
PRA IL TRIVMPHALE VEHICVLO.ET POLIA ETPOLI
PHILOAMBOLIGATI DRIETOSEQVENTI, CVMMA-
XIMOTRIVMPHO ALLA PORTA DILMI-
RABILE AMPHITHEATRO PERVE-
NERON.ILQVALE,ETFORA,
ETINTROPLENAMEN-
TEELLOILDISCRI
VE.

VAVEMENTE CVM MITE AVRASPI-
rante zephyro uibrate molliculamentc ledecore &au
ree pinnule dil diuino puello,& cum il fuo tranquillo
fpirito uehente al refluo littore peruenuti molte & in fi
nite femidee dorophore,& infigne nymphe, cum per-
fpicua pulchritudine,exeunti nui dilla fatale nauicu-
la.Dirincontro pftamente,al diuino ,&aligero puero,cú agregario agmi
ne,cú magno apparato di ornamenti,& di pompe,& fumptuofi ueftimé
ti,cum diuo fafto & culto,piu che regio,cum exquifitiffimo exornato p-
cipue & folemneméte uenerante,di tenera, & florentiffima ætatula q̃ iucundiffime pyrriche, cum uirginei alleétabuli,& cœlefti ,& illuftri afpe-
éti humilmente,&cum decentiffimo famulitio obfequiofe tute fe dapati
ce offerirono.Et ante tute le thereutice paftophore,pyrgophore , &le anti
ludie iubiláte pcedeuano ,cum trophæi di militare decoramenti in hafta
di oro ficilitate difpofiti,cum la thoraca dil furiale Pyroente, cum laltre
armature deuiéte, & cum larco tranfuerfariamente pendice retiné-
te la thoraca, & cú la fpiculata pharetra & fecure alle extremi
tate di larco inuículate, & fotto la thoraca explicato lo
rete,cum una fubieéta facie di puerulo alata , &
gemía,& uno pomo fuffixo alla facia nella hafta per medio traieétáte,& nella fummitate la ftellata galea.

* * * * *
* * *
*

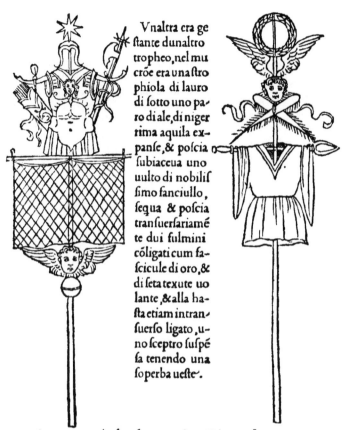

Vnaltra era ge
ftante dunaltro
tropheo, nel mu
cróe era una ftro
phiola di lauro
di fotto uno pa-
ro di ale, di niger
rima aquila ex-
panfe, & pofcia
fubiaceua uno
uulto di nobilif
fimo fanciullo,
fequa & pofcia
tranfuerfariamé
te dui fulmini
cóligati cum fa-
fcicule di oro, &
di feta texute uo
lante, & alla ha-
fta etiam intran-
fuerfo ligato, u-
no fceptro fufpé
fa tenendo una
foperba uefte.

Gerula era ancora ùnaltra duno trophæo. Di una galea, cum uno capo
bubalo, & di fotto una toraca antiquaria, cum dui fcuti per fingulo exito
brachiale connodati, Tra gliquali due fafciole una per lato perpendeuáo
penfile tenente la cleonea pelle, cùm la umbilicata & glandulofamente to
rofa claua.

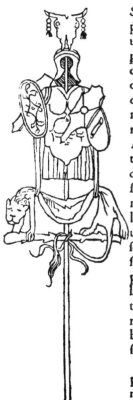

Subſequéte & una attolleua uno tropheo cū ꝑcipua politura. In uno mucrone demigra ua il ſuꝑmo haſtile, ſubdeſcendédo uno co ptorio ſopra una rotunditate ſemiſextante craſſa, i modo platineo reſupinaua, nel me diano inſculpta una formula circinata. La quale uno pauculo di uaſeo pediculo ſuppri meua. Poſcia una tabella cum tale ſcriptura maiuſcula (QVIS EVADET ?) ſubiaceua. A queſta uno pomulo ſubigeua, & ſubſequé te unaltra rotun datione, quale la ſuperna, ma mi nore. Da uno a lamento circū uallata & ad una ſolida ouero ma ſſicia ſcutella ſu peraſſidéte. Dal laquale cōtinua to deſcendeua u no longiuſculo baluſto, & po ſcia una pileta.

Similmente portaua unaltra nympha una ha ſta. Nellacumi nato era una figura ouola, cum orulo bul lato in circinao, & nel meditullo uno rotun damento ſaphyreo la figura imitante di craſ ſitudine unciale, ſubaꝗta una aſſula, tale cum titulo. NEMO. Et in medio di due ale, la ha ſta alquanto balluſticata intraieꝗaua. Inſi mamente una ſcutella ſequiua, quale ſopra e recenſito.

Conſequéte

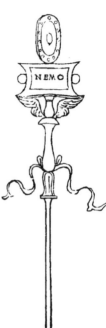

Confequente era uno altro nobiliſſimo trophæo baiulato. Nel ſublime haſtile una pila ſopra uno pyrronio promineua tra uno iflexo lunario di due pinne ſubtilmẽte di braɛ́tea d'oro foliate, uno folio paginataméte ſo pra laltro ſoppſ ſo. Il reſiduo dil lequale in circi naméto coaɛ́to rendeua una co rona cũ faſceo la detenta, p me dio la haſta exi guaméte balau ſtata traieɛ́tan do perpendicu larm̃te. Sotto la corona una pi leta, cum il fun do di uno gut- turnio uaſo de- ſcendéte ſopra il ſmigio di due coniunɛ́te ale-. dapoſcia una fi gura ouolata cũ una bulla byſſi na nel umbili- co corruſcante. Sotto queſta infixa era una pila peponaceam̃te ſcindulata, cum uolan- te faſcicule opportunam̃te inſtriɛ́te-.

Molti altri diplixo narrato gli ſtyraci de liquali alcuni di Hebeno, altri di ſandalo ru bente citrino & bianco , & di candidiſſimo Ebure, & aurati, & di argen- to conteɛ́ti, & di altri pretioſi lignamini. Omni coſa fabre deformata di tenuiſſimo oro, argento, & di leuigata materia, & di ſeta uirente formati & di omni altra gratioſa coloratione, cum iucunda floratura. Cum gemme multiplicemente ornati agli congruenti lochi omni coſa harmonicamé te deſtinata & conſpicuamente applicata, cum præpendenti ſpondili, o-

x

uero uerticuli di ꝑtioſe petre ꝑtuſati, traducto per gliquali filamento aureo, & omni coſa requiſitamente cum iucúdiſſimo coloraṁto depictura
ta , & cum ſcitillante illuſtratióe ſplendicante, & le geſticulatrice inchiro-
tecate di chiroteche cum acuale textura in multiplici noduli & floruli di
filatura aurea & argentea, & di ſeta di uario coloramine artificioſaṁte có
texte, cum crumenale concluſura in uno phrygiolo dialitho agli roſei, &
carnoſi brachii , cum cordicule auree cófuſe uenuſtamente di uaria colo
ratione di ſeta elegante congeſteˊ.

Præiua tutte queſte trophigere una euulſa & exprópta ̦ la uexillationeˊ
dilla nauicula geſtatrice cú prompta gerulatione procurreua . Et immediate imitaria ſequiua unaltra, cú una triumphale celibari, laquale nel ſupremo haueua uno alato Cupidine & diſuelaminato in acto cú larcho
pectente calcaua uno pomo, nel ſupremo inflexo duna gioia di foliatio-
ne laurina di bractea . Laquale era ſupra uno fundo íuerſo di gutturnio
uaſo. Et quiui illaqueata era ̦ le faſceole lambéte di ſupra lo interſtitio dilla gioia extra burriuano uolante . Intro il contento dil circulo era una
tabella, ꝑ lacraſſitudine dillaquale la haſta terebraua, & ꝑ una pila, alla tabella, nella mediana parte extrinſeca ſuperaſſidente, & cuſi nella ſua parte ima unaltra ſubiacente penetraua . Similmente nello abacato di ambi
dui & læuo & dextro lato proſiluaalquanto di haſtula tranſacto ꝑ la gioia, & fora promineua. Dalluno & dalaltro ̦pminente pendici erano dui
funiculi intorti di oro & di ſerico ̦ per bache di ꝑtioſe petre traiectato.
Sotto il riuexo dilla gioia, uno gutturnio uaſo cum il fundo ſuper
nate ſubigeua, & lo orificio in balauſtica aptione, una figura o-
uolata mordicaua cú liniamenti imitanti la forma. Cum
dui pomuli ſupra la circúferentia uno per lato, nel me
dio diametrale, nel imo unaltra pila. Poſtrema-
méte uno nextrulo aureo cum uariata te
xtura uolitante. Nella tabella da u-
na & laltra facie era di maiuſcule græce tale titu.
lo . ΔOΡΥ-
ΚΤΗΤΟΙ.

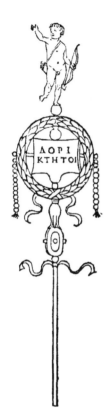

Et molti altri falerati cum molto polimine
di uarii flori.fronde.& fructuli,nó fencia fo
tiatione di bractee doro,& argéto,& di omni
coloramento enchaufticamente infecte, cú
infiniti ornamini & exquifita elegátia di politura,progrediente lætiffime,cum altre affai
infigniture & uictoriale notule,& di exuuie
& fpolie & manubii trophæali decoramenti,
& dal potente & diuino fanciullo fagittabon
do,deuicte pcedéte cum moderata diftantia
di triumphale proceffo,& cú molto plaufo
& diuo thiafo,& cum foni & gutturiali tubi
li dille pheretrie geftante.

Dapofcia prima aprefentatouife la fua diua
uxore Pfyche,cú regilla uefte, cum fulciúto
uillofo,& chermeo oro colluftrante di textu
ra aurea triliciata & tramata,di lucente ferico
iduta.Quale Hermaria & malicha di Hefpe
ria non pduceno.Et fubfequente le comite
di fericie uefte di difcreta & uerficolore ifectu
ra laute & genialeméte indute,cú habiti fupbi
inuifitati & noui,opulentiffimamente di ali-
thi.Quali la natura noftra ad gli humani í-
gegni nouercamente fare interdice,cuim cri-
fpule pliche rugofamente fopra gli delicati &
q̃ mundiffimi corpufculi,& fopra li uergina
le anche,al fuaue impulfo dille frefche aure
inquietule.

Alcune cum inhærenti pectorali di fqua-
mea o peratura aurea,cum uenufto & fotiale ornato di lucentiffime gem-
me.Et altre gli albiffimi pecti,piu che le hyberne pruine di Capricorno
inducti haueano gli affettati ueftimenti,cum decoramento & delicie dil
primo tuberare dille indomite mámillule,quale omelli orthomaftici cú
femi glomulo porrecte & affixe,fopra di effe fina al pectorale cincto inco
lore cyaneo de pilo incochleaua uno fumptuofo phrygio fuffarcinato di
orientale perle,alquanto tuberulante occupaua dapaticamente tutta la
diaphragma,ouero tutta quella parte fupra il cinctorio di artificiofi uolu
ti,di egregia foliatura,quale nunque in Phrygia dagli phrygioni fue inué
to.Et in colore phœniceo,aliquantulo quella incochleatura di uernanti

tra affula gemmale appéfa era una oblóga ouero ouola,tutte di mira craffitudine. Il phrygio dilla fecunda tra le margarite in forma hemiale erano
tabellule di pollicaria longitudine & di femi la latitudine,interuallate tra
due circulare,& dapofcia tra due quadre,cum altri additamenti di lapilli,
negli uacui uenuftaméte appachi & di ornaculi ad delitia & gratia optima
mente inferti,da obftupire effa natura,cum iugi fulgetri plucétiffimi ful-
guranti,& di conuenientia dil coloramine iucundiffimi,cú le maniche

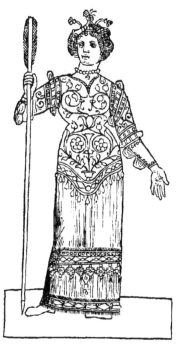

bellissime , & fuperbi brachiali
cú ornato thoracale,Et allo exi
to brachiale & al collare di tali
recenfiti phrygii ,& ornati cir-
cundauano belliffime.Gli bra
chii bipartitamente erano inte
chi dallo exito fina al cubito ,&
dal cubito fina alla comphen-
fa dilla mano era el manicheto
di tuta aurea textura, cum eximie operature fumiffe cótexto
circúuallato duno phrygiolo
di nympheale ftudio diligente
mente inuento nella diuifione
cubitale bellule illaqueati , cú
cordilli aurei,ouero cum intor
tuli funiculi. Nelle diuifione
era uno elegáte exito di copio
fo grumulo cum curuamine
compliculato dilla bóbicia ni
uea tenuiffima & nitente inte-
rula,nella parte decente inuinculati,cum fericei laqueoli ge-
minati in armilete, ouero in or
biculi aurei complanati intro
meffi,& di puro oro mucrona-
ti,cum noduli pendenti cum exquifito uirgiale.Perche quiui il defio ,&
cupito cum il fapere & potere conciliauafe cum la uoluntate.Tanto me
Iupiter ad gli amorofi ochii ǭ iucundiffimo, che altro ueramente nó fe
defiderarebbe,cha perpetuo potere mirare,& fi uenufte , & di formofitate
& di delitia , Nymphe præftante cum gli afpechi elicopidi tanto laute , &
lafciuaméte decore,& tale cum niuee uefte cú fúma politione ṗnitente.

                                                Cum

Cum tanta prouocatione,che allaſpra morte lo homo ultroneamēte ſe
offeriſca & uoléte. O contagioſo artificio. Qallectiuo miniſterio,O pro
pugnante machine. Qualūque core ſano tutiſſimo,ualido & quieto,& li
bero,& renitente,di facilmente inficere,repente di ſubuertire & depopula
re,ſencia mora proſternere,ſencia induſio perturbare,totalmēte ſubiuga
re,& ſencia relucto trahere. Di proſtrare diſcuſſamīte omni moderata , in
credibile & peruicace continentia. Queſti ſono quegli ueraci & infallibi
li ſateliti dil operoſo amore cū ampliabile numero di immaniſſimi car
nifici ,le immune remote,& diſiuncte penſiculatione inſidianti ,& da ta
le inclinante ſubiectione excluſi di potere per alcuno modo,ne cum au
dente aío preualerſe,& dalle pſentate ineuitabile,& trahente dulcitudine,
cum táto ſolerte & diligente ſtudio illaqueabile,& cū ſubtile ingegnio i
uento tanto exquiſitiſſimo operamento & ad tanto bella & formoſiſſima
opera per ſe dalla fœcunda natura,artificio da diſtrugere ritrouato,& exi
mio adiuncto & acceſſorio di cruciare. Ome ilquale ragioneuolmente
fingere ſe douerebbe,& uſare per le marmoree ſtatue,& non per gli huma
ni & fragili cori. Imperoche ancora quel nobile & diuo ſexo , ſpoliato &
denudato ſummaínte contorque & inſice periclitabondi, Non che cum
queſto uoluptico additaméto di laquei pernitioſo inueſtigato. Ma ſolo
queſto accede,che elle non penſiculano eſſere aſſai il damore naturalmé
te perire,ſencia tanto aucto incremēto di excogitati modi adiúgere gli mi
ſeri & molliculi amanti allo interito dil cordolio piu facilmente di con
ducere,& continuamente excitare ſcintillule extremamīte incendioſe da
uegetare alla conſumptione le amoroſe & feruide flammule,diui obiecti
di rimpire & confundere il caldo pecto di bullienti ſuſpiruli,& di fermen
tare il core adamore. Hora io non ſaperei debitamente exprimere p quale
modo uno táto fundamine iacto damore ſtabile & ſincero fermamente
in Polia collocato,che alquáto quaſſare il ſentiſſe da queſte ineuitabile &
parate inſidie & impetuoſe uiolentie. Ome poſcia tra me tacitamīte repli
caua. O prophilea Pollia bellatula mia,cuſtodi la tua adepta pda. Impero
che grande periclitamīto,e il tranſito p tante pyratice fallacie ,& manifeſti
ſicarii & pdonuli íſidiarii. Gli quali contra oi ſincera rectitudine ſono dil
ſuo amoroſo offēdimine cómēdati & laudabilmīte approbati & dagli tri
ſti offenſi,táto piu deſiderati & riuerētemīte piu reqſiti & piu dolce amati.

Hora nella ſua lætiſſima fronte,ſotto a due hemicycle,quale filo di ſeta
ſubtile,& nigerrime ciglie piu che illuſtrante electro ,dui ſagittabondi o
chii feſteuolmīte luceuano piu che irradiátiſſime ſtelle nel lympidiſſimo
cœlo ſplendeſcēte. Et nel aſpecto ſuo piu belle che incarnate,& ricente ro
ſe,& le gene nó miltate, ma cú piu gratiſſima & genuía rubedie,che degli

meli decii nel uinifero autūno uermigliáte &piu lucide c̄il biáchiſſimo
eburo pfricato ,oue il Sole ſe dimóſtraua piu chiaro forſa che tale ad gli a-
chiméiiTitáo nó appariſſe. Et ad gli ægyptii oſiride,ouero Iſide,ouero ſe
rapi cū il Calatho ,ouero tricipiti ſimulacro·Et nel ſacro AntroInitra ad
gli pſii,q̄le exponeuaſe nelladuéto dil ſuo ſignore le delitioſe & diuenym
phe Cū uenerandi ſembiáti conſpicue, cum ornati geſti morate & mori-
gere,cum non uiſitata bellecia ſpectatiſſime, Et cum p̄ſtante ligiadria exi
mie,cum elegante honeſtate p̄clare & decore,& cum integra procacitate
ornate & comptiſſime.

Ad queſto punĉto meritamente cum ueneranda caterua ualante , &
cum frequente comitato proſequente la beliſſima Pſyche gratificabon-
da riuerendo il Cariſſimo Marito tutta ageuola & blandicella riceuete,&
cum ſummo uenerato,nel capo una pretioſiſſima corolla poſeli ,che tale
non fue la uotiua di Hiero. Et due dille Nymphe eſſa honorabonde co-
mitante Imeria una,Polia placidamente riceuete. Et laltra Erototimoride
facetiſſima ,& me per lamano app̄ſe . Dapoſcia diſtinĉtamente ſequendo
molte altre lætiſſime trine & trine,cum ſoléne proceſſo,& ordine , & ho-
norificentiſſima pompa,& decente ueneratione,& cum nymphale geni-
culatione ormomene ueneron·

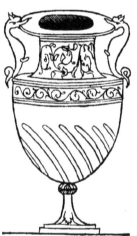

Et primo uene Toxodora, Laquale
il ſinuato,& uulnifico arco accortamen
te gli offeriua.Ilquale rigoroſamente era
extento. Queſta era in medio di due al-
tre.Ennia una,che nelle tuberule mano
gerulaua uno dedolato uaſculo Am-
phoe di coloriſſimo ſaphyro cum iu-
cundiſſima ſplendeſcentia ,cum latulo
orificio emuſicatamente exſcalpto .Dal
quale alquantulo di cliuulo di multipli
ce florato cum maxima politura expreſ
ſo ,alla dilatata corpulentia moderatam̄
te deſcendeua , ſopra lo initio dil graci-
larſe dalla tornata corpulatura receden-
te uerſo lo orificio leanſule adhæreſcen
te ,in uipeo effigiato diligentiſſime deformate. Il limbo elegantemente gulu-
lato mordicauano . Dapoſcia il circū-
cinĉto corpuleſcente nelextriſeco di mi
ri ſimulachruli cœlato, & p̄politulam̄te cófiĉto,& oue il corpulam̄to í-
cominciaua demigrare inanguſtia dil gracile &oblongo fundo , era di

canaliculi obliquifcenti, cum moderati riuuli inalueati excauato , fini-
uano fupra uno nodulo,cum temperato tumore al folerte reperto ,cum
uno fubacto pedulo ,ftipato di belliffimi & multiplici flori,quegli diffe-
minante. Et la fua conforte Phileda nel gremio ricoglieua quello che E-
nia folatiofamente fpargendo diffeminaua.

Similmente tra due altre ornatiffime nymphule fe fece ananti Ve-
lode,Quefta al fuo fignore feftiuamte gli aprefentoe una mirabile pharetra fuperba di artificio & di inuento egregio,cum due uelociffime fagit
te, Vna cum il ftrale di puro argento,& laltro cum il pontuto ftrale di negro ,graue,frigido & infaufto plumbo.Ad quefto & dicio ello il fuo tene-
ro ,& diuino fiancho, ouero gli armi dille uolante arme fe pcingeffe , &
le compare Omonia & diapraxe,cum due pile lætabonde iocauano,lu-
na allaltra alternantile . Ma di lucido oro era quella di Omonia , & di
fragile cryftallino haueala fua Diapraxe, Et quando una di effe repiglia-
ua quella di oro ,rimandaua la cryftallina,cum folerte uitato di obuio i-
feme.

Ad quefte pofcia ordinariamente & le altre fubfequiuano la belliffima & riuerente Typhlote,cu religiofi & demeriti honori & dignificatio-
ne,Ella uno tenuiffimo uelamine offerite cernua, Ad quefto che gli fue
lati ochii lui gli doueffe teniare & rico prire.Quefta haueacum fe due la-
fciue damicelle,cum impudico fembiante.Dillequale una Afynecha no
minata rotantife,mo al lato dextro,modo al finiftro inconftante & Arde
lia Comazifta ballaua.Et quale Thimele Hiftrionica faltante ioculatrice
& lamia infigne.

Et laltra Afchemofyne tra tutte le ueftite nuda imperterrita ,& falace
faprefentoe . Ne piu ne meno fi dal fonte Salmacide potata fuffe. Et in
lamano finiftra una fphæra formata di lamine auree, cum il fuo centro
teniua . Et cum la dextera blandamente il longo capillamento appren-
fo extenderfi fupra le polpofe & criffate nate ,non confentiua,cum in ue
reconda petulantia,Quale petulca qftulatrice , ma indicando Tribaba
obfcæniffima infolentia cum extollentia di gliochii inconftanti & cefii,
& cum pruritofo acto,Quale procace gaditana, cum troppo lafciuien-
tia infabre geftiente,& piu chel fpurciffimo hoftio in fe non hebbe , nel
fpeculare gli drauci & gli caui fpeculi.

Nouiffimamte tre altre i pmeditabode matrone fapfentorono,Telefte la
pria, di ardete purpura iduta,cum gli foluti & pmiffi capilli ,& nella ftro-
phiata frote crifpatuli ppedeti,effa elegate al fuo idio gli dete una accefa
facola,& una comitate Vrachiuia gerula dauafe di una fmeragdina urnu

la faberrimaméte expreſſa,& antiquario artificio,& inſoléte auſo ſi da hu
mana opatura.Lo orificio haueua contortamente ſtriato,lequale ſtrie,o
uero riuuli nella mediana amplitudine dil uaſo moderatamente finien
do ,cũ æquatiſſima diſtributione alquanto ſe dilatauano.Dapoſcia il ue
nuſto concincto deſcendeua uerſo il rotundo fundo,la corpulentia pau
latinamente exiliſcente,conueſtita cum inextimabile factione di ſelini
cio foliamento ,dal ſolido cum egregia diuulſione prominente ,& dagli
labii dillorificio continuati uerſo il ſubcliuo contorquentiſe inexqui
ſita foliatura,due áſule rendeuano cũ mirifico expreſſo,& cũ uno pedu
culo.

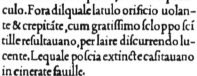

Fora dilquale latulo orificio uolan
te & crepitáte ,cum gratiſſimo ſcloppo ſci
tille reſultauano,per laire diſcurrendo lu
cente.Lequale poſcia extincte caſitauano
in cinerate fauille.

Laltra comite Capnolia uno uaſo caprú
culo,ouero teſtaceo geſtaua,cũ águſto ori
ficio & altiuſculo leuato & attenuátiſe nel
ſudo,& ſopra il ſuo dilatamie ſotto le áſu
le circularmente haueua,cũ æquadiſtantia,
tredeci litere græce menſuratiſſime diligé
temente impreſſe. ΓΑΝΤΑ ΒΑΙΑ ΒΙ
ΟΥ. cum molti altri ornamini & obli-
quanti alueoli.Ilquale dalle litere uerſo lo
orificio era polytrito. Fora dilquale & per
gli ſpiramenti profiliua uno nebulante &
euodio fumo in nulla per laire riſoluen
tiſe.

Recepte

Recepte finalmente le oblate mysterio‑
se & fatale erotenara & conuenienti gesta‑
mini·Il diuino puello ad sedere se pose so
pra uno aureo & antiquario carpento , o ‑
uero uectabulo iui triúphale pparato , tut
to di lamine doro per tutte le fimbrie cir‑
cúambiéte uno phrygio dodráte in latitu
dine. Nel quale solariamente luceuano in
claustrate ostentuose géme di granditudi‑
ne & inopinabile ptio, & di artificio imp‑
ceptibile & di inuento rarissime, diuinam
te disposito, & ordinatamente destinato .
cum due uehiculare rote habente la circú
ferentia doro, & gli radii pcedenti dal cen
trico axe, nel quale il polo iaceua , & infi‑
xi nel meditullio erano deformati longi‑
usculi in balaustico figmento di petre pre
tiose uarie di coloramento fulgurante˜.

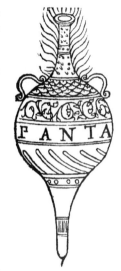

SEDENDO dúque ello sencia protra‑
cto di tempo prensi & capti ambi dui fussimo, Polia, & io dalle præstante
nymphe Plexaura & Ganoma, per lo imperatorio nuto dil triumphan‑
te puellulo dominante, & reiecte da retro di ambi dui le brace , & al tergo
restricte le mane, come captiui Polia & io fussimo illaqueati & uincti, cú
trece & serticuli di rose & uario floramine connexi & resticulati . Et retro
alla pomposa, & diuiata rheda dil athlophoro , & maximo triumphato‑
re eramo tracti molliculamente uoluntabondi da Synesia nympha præ
stantissima.

Perlaquale cosa incomminciai quasi di trepidare. Ma per che le nym‑
phe cum la mia cosmodea Polia facetamente si rideuano di subito me as‑
sicurai. Sequiua immediate dapo nui la curiosa Psyche. Et retro lei erano
sequace le puere damicelle, che uenerante haueuano offerto. Laquale
Psyche era patagiata, ouero superinduta di culto matronale & ambitio‑
sissimo manto doro ouero chlamyda, che tale a Dario non donoe Silosó
te. Ne cusi facta Numa re primo iuétore pote usare. Supra lo humero dex
tro cóplicatulamte iniecta & i orbiculi suppssi doro ansulata, oue tra cras
si carbóculi purgatissimi paragonii, & di splédore corruscáti teniua iclau
strato uno adamáte sesqdigitale lógitrorso & cóplanato, & i latitudíe po
licari, & di ferríeo seitillare, cópleto di mirádo stupore, cú iextimabile de
coramto pminéte, che di tato ptio nó sue da Gige il dono dato ad Apolli

culatiōe incedéte,& di tanto fúptuofo & fupbo triũpho ,& di táte delitie´
& amœnitate,& immenfa amplitudine di p̄tiofe diuitie & maxime opulé
tie piu præfto,che dalla natura, diuine agli ochii mei p la Cythareida gĩa
& cupidineo priuilegio palefemente di uidere,& chiaro & realmente mirare præcipuamente indulto.

Nel ultimo loco immediate ,dinanti
proximo gli trahenti ferpi, dui ægipani,
& procaci fatyri,cum hircino barbitio,
cum gli caprei ,& bifulci pedi procedeua
no.Cliquali petulci lætabundi,cum ftro
phiole di florido fatyrione ,& di flori di
Helenio & di Cynoforchi fupprimente´
gli incópti capili fopra la caperata fron -
te icoronati. Ciafcuno geftaua uno mó-
ftro rudemente excifo in ligno , & inaura
to ,effigiato humano ueftito. Dal tricapo
fina alla diaphragma folamete il refiduo
in quadrato acuminátife alla parte infernate,demigraua in una gulatura bafiale,
cum uno lataftrello , cum una atiq̃ folia
tura nel fito brachiale,cum uno p̓omo al
pecto. Et nel medio dil quadrato nella
parte piu lata appareua lo ithyphallio fi-
gno.

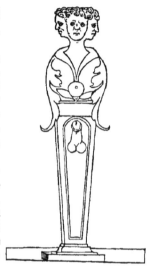

Dinanti agli quali præcedeua immediate una politula nympha ,nel
uolto niueo dillaquale le gene porphyriace rubeuano,cú la hederata fron
te di corymbi,induta di fegmentato palio , uibrati de q & de li da fuaui re
flati zephyrei,gli lacinii dil reflato fino,baiulaua uno uafculo aureo ,in
modo di papila rotundato,lacte p anguftiffimo meato afpgendo libaua.

Similmente ancora due nymphe p̄cedente redimite luna di folii dilla fœmina Linozofte,& laltra di Hermopoane mafculo ,erano geftatrice.
La una di uno integro puerulo inaurato nella dextra , Et nelaltra uno al
tro dil capo,brachioli, & dil collo mutilato. Laltra cum p̄cipuo honore
& obftinata fupftitione el fimulachro dagli ægyptii di Serapi uenerato
portaua. El quale era uno capo di leone . Alla dextra profiliua uno capo
di cane blandiente. Et dalla læua,uno capo di rapace lupo. Laquale effigie era tuta in uno uolumine di draco contenta & circundata,radii præa
cuti emittéte. Il quale draco cum la tefta alla dextra parte del fimulacro de
riuaua faberrimamente deaurato.

Onde

Onde cum emusicata distantia ,&cum
longo & soléne progresso ,comitato era il
triumphante fanciullo,& ambidui Polia
& io inuinculati di florenti serticuli &ui-
minali rosei festabondi. Le nymphe di fa-
ceta natura molto benignamente actiue
a nui gratificantise amorosi blandimenti
prolectante saceuano,cum festiui uolti &
genuina hilaritudine,& amoroso solami
ne pmulcente.

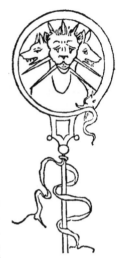

Finalmente cum questo triumphale
& mysterioso discorso, & cum le pheretrie pompe&amorose niciterie, tra rido-
lenti flori successiuamente procedendo ,
præcellente la uexillatione dilla insigne
uictoria,cum gli anticantamenti dilla læ
tissima iuuentute nymphale,cum incesso
perfluo &antiludii,&cum corusce face p
lucente &cum chiaro lume præmicante
pcedeuano, Et tra fragrante olere,olente & uiue arbore,odoriseri fructi,o
dorofo aire & clemente & liquidissimocœlo.Sepita la strata cum omni ge
neramento di fruteti consita &in omni parte contecto di herbule,& di
uirente gramine.Non uacando apasso apasso le rose,& la copia di flori,
omni cosa fragrante &loco fœlice,beato,delitioso,&amœnissimo. Et cú
tanta & diua sequétia di turba miscellanea di nymphe,cum peculiare pó
pa,cum religioso progresso immo triumphale,la una dalaltra ,cum statu
ta &determinata distantia comitato incedeua,sotto la rosaria pergula di
omni manera,cum nouelle,& uerne fronde &foglie . Laquale da dolci
strepiti obsibilaua.
Et quiui tutto il solo ubertosamente obruto & coperto era di sternate fo
glie di rose,&di flore naranceo,di amethystine uiole,&matronale luteole
& di bulle albe,&di pulliphure purpurante & di flori di Iosamino di li-
lii &altri conspicui &olentissimi flosculi.Et singularmente era dissemi-
nato il semine,dilla unicaule aristalthea,& ramuli di florente myrto . Sopra lo æquatissimo silicato,di lucentissimi marmori in finite operature tessellataméte compacti. Molte portauano tyrsi di multiplice florami
ne congrumati,Altre cum rami di olea,Alcune di lauro ,molte di myrto,& di altri celebrati arbori cum auicule intrepide familiarmente sopra
assidente cum canora garrulatione & concenti suaui cátante,cum le cá-
y

tante nymphe hymni & cantici,& cum dulcissimi moduli psalléte p ttit
to adsonauano,cum cæleste plauso lætissimamente festigianti cum hila ,
re cerimonie & cum delicato & uirginale tripudio ardeliamente,& alcune cum saltatione pyrrhica,& altisone laude extollendo la diuina genitri
ce & il potente filiolo,cum festiui spectaculi cum maximo triumpho , &
superba pompa paulatinamente pueniffimo ad uno proscenio , oue era
una conspicua ,& faberrima,& scitiffima porta hiante,di materia,& di o-
peratura di uno mirabiliffimo amphitheatro sublime instructo di fabri-
ca,pleno di artificio di ornamenti &arte non uiso mai tale, Ne in Atella
ne in qualúque altro famoso loco exquisitiffimamente fabrefacto & pfe-
ctamente absoluto di lunga narratione explicabile,& quasi non cogitabi
le.Quale dire si potrebbe non humana,ma piu psto diuina operatione,
& ostentamento maximo di structura.

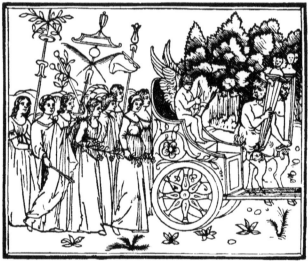

GIVNTI dunque cum sóléniffimo gaudio, & incredibile lætitia, &
solàtioso dilecto per la triumphale uia cum distributa aspergine indi &
quindi per alcune strictiffime auree fistulete, irrorante di odoratiffime
aquule gli proceffionarii,& tutta la triumphatrice turma rosidulamente
pfusa alla porta di lingreffo, mirai che lera stupendo artificio · La quale
constructa era di orientale litharmeno, nelquale infinite scintule , quale
scope disperse se cerniuano di fulguràte oro. Et di questo puro metallo e-
rano

rano dille exacte colúne le bafe,gli capituli. Il trabe . zophoro , coronice, & faftigio limine & ante, & omni altro opamento dilla recen fita materia uedeuafe,renuéte il duro & tenace chalybe & afpernabile la toreuma
ta antiquariamente uariata,gratiofo elegante & fpectatiffimo expreffo , &
ftructura oltra modo magnifica.Laquale io penfo da gli terriculi nó facti
bile,cú fummo i pendio & longanimitate,graue & diutía faticha,& cum
nó mediocre ingegnio,cura & induftria,& diligentia , che ad tale oftento
fuffe abfoluta & ad fabrefacta era nella clufura di tutto larco di ophitea pe
tra,& le collaterale colúne ambe prophyrice. Pofcia laltre uariando, & o-
phitea una,& laltra ꝑphyrica. Le mediane fupaftante alle porphyrite,ábe
ophite,& le fupernate quadrágule mediane di porphyrite,& pofcia con-
trariádo luna allaltra,& cufi ꝑ il contrario mutamine erano capituli bafe
& arule.

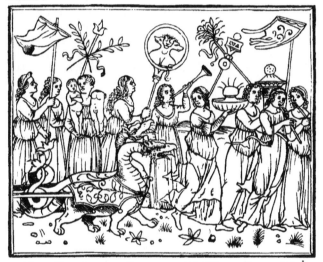

Dinanti laquale uno per lato,era uno ꝓtiofiffimo uafo,uno di faphy-
ro,laltro di fmaragdo,di maximo & obftinato artificio faberrimamente
dædale facti .Penfai degli uafi allingreffo dil téplo di Ioue in Athene col
locati.

A quefta defcripta porta mirabile dil triúphale & uolucre uehiculo il
fignore Arquite difcefe. Lo áphitheatro era di icredibile inuifitata & iau
dita ftructura. Impoche il pedaméto elegante,& gliemuficati concincti,

y ii

ouero illigamenti,& il ſymmetriato colúnio in gyro.Trabi.zophori,&
coronice tutto excluſiue era di conflatura ænea,enchauſticamente obau
rata di fulgurante oro.Il reſiduo tutto di alabaſtryte diaphano,& di col
luſtrante nitella,&le ante cum gli archi ,ouero trabi inflexi. Ne tale opa
M.Scauro fece nella ſua ædilitate.

Il quale dalla parte extima hauea dui æquali ordini di puii archi inter
calati tra le colúne.Vno ordine allaltro ſuppoſito de hemicyclo il ſuo i-
flexo cum lo additaméto. Et tra le apertione degliquali nel ſolido late
perpendicularímte emineuano appaĉte ſemi colúne ſtriate, cum il tertio
ſuo rudentate cum nextruli,ouero reguli.Alcune cum æqua alteratione
& diſtributo referte di ſigni & di imaguncule,quale in Epheſo núque fu
rono uiſe.Suppoſite alle baſe dillequale condecente arule iaceuano,& cú
il requiſito liniamento. Ad gli anguli dillequale appaĉti pédeuano dui
oſſi di capo di ariete,uno di q,& laltro dilli,cú gli rugoſi corni ícochlea
ti,ouero cum intorta uertigine, p lequale uſciuano certe cymoſe inſeme
innodate,una frondea gioia cum ſuppſſo foliamento ,& di prominenti
fruĉti retinente & illaqueante,nel contento dilla undulatione quadrata
dilarula. Dentro il capo dilla gioia egregiamente exſcalpto era uno ſa
crificulo ſatyrico,cum una aruletta ad uno tripode ſubieĉta cum uno eo
culo antiquario bulliente,& due nude nymphe,una per lato,cum una fiſtuletta nel foco flante,& proximo alarula dui pueruli uno per lato,cum
uno uaſculo p uno.Similmente & dui laſciui Satyri cum indicio di uoci
ferare,cum uno pugno ſtriĉtamente uerſo le nymphe leuato,cum i
trichatione anguinea.Lequale cum il libero brachio branchia
ti quelli degli ſatyri,gliquali cum la máo dillaltro brachio lo
rificio di uno uaſo futile obturauano prohibiuano il ta-
ĉto,& inclinate cumlaltro teniuano la fiſtuletta al ſuo
officio intente & immote.Alcune altre colum
ne di queſta medema forma,cum gli dui
tertii di alueatura torqueata,& lo infi
mo arulato come e diĉto,mutaua-
no geminate di liniamento.Ta-
le haueuáo tra tuberate reſte-
di fróde & fruĉti ícurue-
ſcéte pueruli ludibódi.
Alcune multipli ci tro
phæi ſcalpture egregiamte faĉte
molte haueuáo exſcalpte cógerie di exuuie.
Altre occupati di ſigni appaĉti plaudéte dee ,&
puelluli & uiĉtorie copie & tituli & altri ornamti cógruétiſſimi.

Sopra gli fúmi fca
pi fuper affideuano
gli eximii capituli
dille recenfite colú
ne cú artificiofi aba
chi , ouero opculi
fotto le extenfure,
degliquali fubfide-
uano le perpolite
helice magiore , lo
illigamento trabeo
& di phrygio & co
ronatione circinã-
te, cum le proiectu
re dil uiuo cógrua-
mente a perpendi-
culo dille colúne.

Tra una proiectu
ra & laltra ,nel ordi
ne dilla porta nella
parte mediana dil
zophoro, conftaua
artificiofamte expf
fo uno nobiliffimo
excogitato, & inué
to di ueterrimo ua-

fo ftipato hauédo lo orificio di antiquarie & ppendente fronde.Et de qui
& deli iaceua uno cornuto boue pftrato cum gli pedi protéfi al uafo,& cú
il capo eleuato, & uno nudo quello æquitante cú la dextera elata,& im-
pugnato multiplice uirgule,idicaua p cu ffuro ,cum laltra il paleario collo amplexando. Proximo ilquale una fanciulla nuda dorfuariamente fe
deua,cú il brachio uerfo il folido áplexaua il nudo fopra le pátice,& cum
laltra rapito teniua uno uelante páno di fopra uia il uittato capo i pedito
fotto il fuo federe ufciua per fopra il brachio áplexáte,in pfpecto uno fatyro,il corno abrácato dil boue cú lítima mano,& cú laltra uoltato il tergo al boue ,leuata uerfo la dóna teniua uno íglobato ferpe.Détro unaltro
fatyro,cú una mano allaltro corno ritinuto fe cum laltra rapiua p gli lori
una pédéte grauidatura di fróde cógerate riuexa fopra lo imo dil corpula
méto dil uafo diffiniua, pofcia cú moderata icuruefcétia allincótro nella

y   iii

mano dillaltro satyro. La parte posteriora degli boui migrãte uerso le prominentie ĩ nobilissime spire di antiquarie fronde transformauase. Per q̃sto medemo mõ uariando il zophoro uenustamẽte ĩscalpto era decorato.

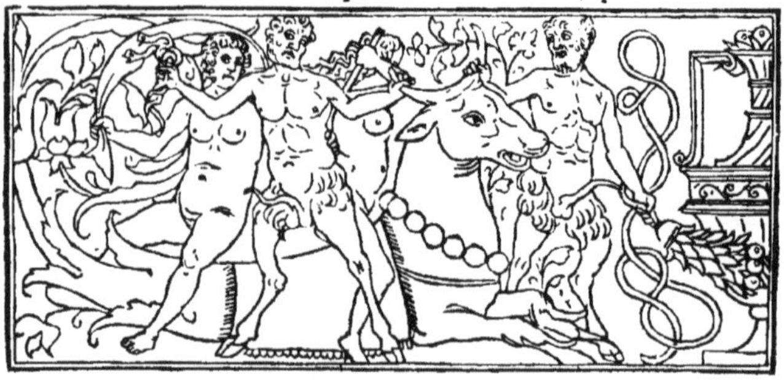

Vltra questo primario illigamẽto sequiua ascendendo ordinatamẽte uno simigliante di colũne in omni cosa cõueniente & in niuna parte discrepãte. Et quãtũque larte ædificamẽtaria appetisca che le super apposite colũne piu breue il quarto dille substitute essere debono, dille quale il perpendiculo deueniua sencia lo arulato supra el centro dille subdite cũ la sequẽtia. Et le tertie il quĩto. Niente di meno ĩ questo elegante, & symmetriato ædificamẽto, questo nõ era obseruato, Ma di una ꝑceritate, & le superna te cũ le inferne. Le tertie quadrãgule nel tertio ordine obediuano. Haueuano ancora queste sup assidẽte colũne lo illigamẽto ambiente, quale le subiecte. Vltra questa cõcĩctura, le quadrãgule, ouero pilastrelli sulcati sa liuano. Et tra uno & laltro dal solido uno suo tertio euulse, nella æq̃ta ĩter capedine hiaua una finestra, non quadrãgula al modo templario, ma q̃le e requisito nelle ꝓfane ædificature obliquate, ouero inarcuate.

Supmamẽte in orbe gyrato sopra le quadrate colũne, la regia coronice sencia ꝓiecture, cum omni ornato & requisitissimo liniamento & cum il ꝑcipuo ĩ essa douuto suggrundio, cũ omni proportione harmonica circũligaua. Oltra la dicta, sublato circinaua uno nitido & expedito alamẽto alto uno passo & semisse.

Tutto q̃sto celebre. illustre. supbo. & sũmamẽte apꝓbato ædificamẽto di finissimo alabastryte ĩdico, di uitrio nitore artificamẽte cõstructo optimamẽte decorato, & egregiamẽte absoluto sencia illimẽto di calice pulte. ouero cemẽto, ma cũ stabile cohæsiõe & cõtracto cõsenso ꝑfecto. Laq̃le ꝑnitẽte materia nõ era dedignata da maculabile fumo, nõ palescẽte perunctura di olio illibuta, ne lutea ꝑ ĩfusione di uermigliaceo uio, ma ĩ oĩ parte obnoxia sencia alcuna ĩfectiõe, nella sua nitella superba. luculẽta riseruato. La

Area continiua per diametro paffi.xxxii.La craffitudine dilcompofito
paffi octo.

La partitione dilla columnatione ambiente,era quadrifaria diuifa fo
pra la circunferentia.Tra una & laltra partitione interiecte conftauano
cum æqua difcriminatione octo diuifure,oue conftituite & appofite era
no le columne.Dalle quale il folido uerfo il centro procedeua, Et per il
recto,& per circuitione tranfuerfarie incircinao,extauano commenfu-
ratamente le fuffulture columnarie,Tra una & laltra partitaméte gli hia
ti dille apertione,correfpondentifi linialmente peruii, & interuacui, Et
artificiofaméte teftudinati gli portici o uero fornici, Le linee anguftian
tife cum mira conuenientia,Le recte & le circinante tranfuerfale laltitu
dine referuata,& omni normico alla harmoniaaccefforio. Il pauimen-
titio folo,era egregiaméte fecticio di iuéto mirabile & di arte cófpicuo,

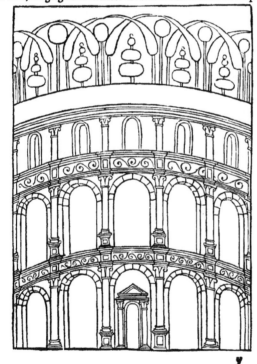

y *iiii*

Dalquale apprefentati fuffimo dinanti al facro fanĉto fonte cyth ereo.

POLIPHILO IL MIRABILE ARTIFICIO DIL VENEREO
FONTE DESCRIVE NEL CENTRO DILLA THEATRA
LE AREA EXISTENTE, ET COME FRACTA FVE LA
CORTINETTA. ET VIDE LA DIVINA MATRE IN SVA
MAIESTATE, ET COME ESSA SILENTIO ALLE CAN-
TANTE NYMPHE IMPOSE. DILLEQVALE TRE PER
VNO A POLIA ET ALLVIGLI CONSIGNOE . DAPO-
SCIA CVPIDINE AMBI DVI GLI FERITE, ET LA DEA
CVM LAQVA DIL FONTE GLI IMBRE FECE,
ET POLIPHILO FVE REVESTITO.
POSTREMO VENENDO MAR
TE IMPETRATA LA LICEN
TIA SE PARTIRONO.

VM DECENTISSIME VENERATIONE ET
fumma honorificentia la Eutrapela Polia & io affeĉtuo-
famente dinanti al myfteriofo fonte dilla diuina genitrice congenulati, io da una imperceptibile dulcedine dif-
fufamente inuadere uexabonda me fentiua, che in quel
punĉto che fare non fapeua: Impero che per lo amœnif-
fimo & incredibilmente delitiofo fito, & ultra omni credito dileĉtofo di
uirentia & uernale decoramento. Et per le auicule per il puriffimo aere di
fcorrendo, & per le nouelle frōde garriendo uolante ad gli forifeci fenfi, q̃
iucundiffime, & cum le decoriffime nymphe cantante melode infeme
cum gli fui infueti foni audiendo, Et degli fui diui aĉti , & modeftiffime
mouentie uidendo ardentemente impulfo ad extrema uoluptate, & de fi
faĉta fabricatura di tanta dignitate di concepto, & dilla elegantiffima difpofitione folerteméte & curiofo penficulando, & di tanta inexperta fragrantia auidamente hauriendo. Per lo immortale Ioue reĉtamente igno-
raua ad quale fenfituo potere, lo intento obieĉto mio da tanto diuerfo di-
leĉto diftraĉto, & exceffiuo & fœlice folatio & uoluptico placimie firma,
& ftabilmente applicare, & nefcio meaccufaua. Lequale tutte belle, & dul
ciffime cofe tanto piu gratiofo & defiderabile alleĉtaméto ad me allhora
plenamente caufando offeriuano, Quanto che io conofceua la urotio-
thia Polia participe placidaméte delectarfene. In quefto loco, at etiam di
quefto ammirando fonte la nouitate & excellentia mirando.
Ilq̃le

Ilquale nel medioſtimo di queſto in humano ædificamento diuinamĩ
te conſtructo & expreſſo per queſto modo. Della nigerrima petra, che ſo﹣
la integramĩte era tutto il ſilicato, oueramente il pauimentato dilarea di eſ
ſa propria nel mediano in uno murulo ſublato pedale, cum egregia poli
tura reducta cum omni ornato opportuno di forma extrinſeca heptago
no, & della interſtitia rotunda. Cum lambiente cimaſula & ſocco & aru﹣
lette, & undiculatione fabrefacte & ordinariamente ſuppoſite alle baſe, ſo
pra il mediano puncto degli anguli, dilquale per ciaſcuno era ſuper aſtru
cta una entheſiata, ouero uétriculata colúna in numero ſepte, cum ſum﹣
ma exquiſitura turbinate. Dillequale due correſpódeuano æquale ex ad﹣
uerſo dellingreſſo. In conſpecto di queſto oue ſtauamo ‸pni geniculati.

Vna dillequale tornatile colúne, alla dextera parte cyanaua ṗfulgente˒
di finiſſimo ſapphyro, & dalla ſiniſtra uernaua uiréte ſmaragdo di ṗſtan﹣
tiſſimo colore piu lucentiſſimo che gli affixi per gli ochii al Leone al tu﹣
mulo di Hermia regulo. Ne tale fu donato da Ptolemæo ad Lucullo. Ne
di tanta ṗtioſitate fue il ṗſentato da Re di Babylonia al Re Aegyptico, ne
di tanto æſtimamento furono quegli dil obeliſco nel Templo di Ioue˒.
Ne di tanta miraueglia fue la ſtatua nel templo di Hercule in Tyro, quale
queſto admirando ſe ṗſtaua. Proximo ad queſta ſequiua una columna di
petra turchinia di uenuſto Ceruleo coloratiſſima, cum la uirtute gratio﹣
ſamente donata. Et quantúque cæca, Niente di meno illuſtriſſima & ſpe﹣
cularmĩte ṗfulgeua. Contigua al
la ſapphyrica columna aſſideua
una pretioſa di petra cæca etiam
di iucundiſſimo colore, quale il
Meliloto, & di luſtro quale lo i﹣
terlucido floreo dil uatrachio.
Adhæriua a q̃ſta una di Iaſpide˒
di colore hyalino, & laltra di to﹣
patio fulgurante colore aureo. La
ſeptima ſola & ſingularmente era
hexagonia di lympidiſſimo beril
lo indico di oleaceo nitore incó
trario gli obiecti reddendo. Et q̃﹣
ſta per medio dille due prime cor
reſpondeua, per che omni figu﹣

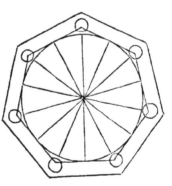

ra diſpare angulare, Vno angulo obuia nel mediano dellintercalato
di dui. Dúque il circulo obducto del ſuo diametro ſemiſſe, iui uno trian
gulo æq̃latero cóſtituito, & poſcia dal cétro una líea, nel medio dilla linea

materia & di opportuni liniamenti elegantissimi significati, nel sedere se
ptúcio & semiassíde nella piana.

Il tessellato alli bella strato fue di tutto lo incluso solo. Il q̃le per omni
parte uirente sencia alcuna denudatione era, & tutto di minutissimo serpillo olente cæsariato, del quale uno solo folio al altro nõ superaua, cú gra
tifica densatura fina alle p̃ripie del fonte uernante contegendo cum æqua
ria tonsura.

Quiui sotto mirai una ueneranda factura. La quale queste diue nym
phe & nui diuotamente reuerissemo uno miraueglioso & di mysterio ple
no staua deputato tale sepulchro pedi quinarii in lógitudine, & in latitudine dextante altra tanto leuato excluso il socco, cum la coronicetta, che
era quincuncio, Il quale tumulo differon le Nymphe essere del uenatore
Adone, in quel loco dal dentato Apro interémpto. Et in questo loco eti
am similmente la Sancta Venere uscendo di questo fonte nuda, in quelli rosarii lancinoui la diuina Sura, per soccorrere quello dal zelotypo Mar
te uerberato cum uultuosa facia & indignata, & cum angore danimo.

Questa tale historietta se uedea perfectamente in scalpta in uno lato p
longo del sepulchro. Et il filio Cupidine recolgière poscia il purpurissi-
mo sangue in uno cortice di Ostrea. Subiungendo che quel diuino cruo
re era reposito in quel sepulchro, cú il cinere, cum omni sancto rito collocato. Di que nel frõte del nostro igresso del sepulchro era excauato cir
cularméte per il capto del quadrato, & obturato, poscia di petra p̃tiosa di
Iacyntho, di colore uermiglio transparente, cum grande corruscatione
di flámeo splendore, p il lume opposito instabile ardendo, che apena ualeua io gli ochii per il uacillamento affirmare.

Dal altro lato p il longo del sepulchro uidi similmente Adone, cum
alcuni pastori uenatore cælati, tra alquanti arbusculi, cum cani & il mor-
to Apro, & esso da quello occiso. Et Venere dolorosamente lachrymabú
da negli pietosi amplexi di tre Nymphe semianime cadeua, di subtilissi-
mo panno indute inseme cum la dea col lachrymauano. Et il filio cum
uno fasciculo di rose gli ochii materni udi di liquante lachryme plora -
bundo tergente.

Quiui tra uno & laltro sexo in una corolla di Myrto uidi cusi inscripto. . IMPVRA SVAVITAS. Per tale modo nel altra historietta in
græco cusi era expresso. ΑΔΩΝΙΑ. Tanto tutte queste cose exquisita
mente di sculptura sicte se præstauano, che io me commoui in una dol-
cecia di pietate.

Il q̃drato dúque opposito a q̃llo del lume p̃pédicularmente deriuaua

sopra

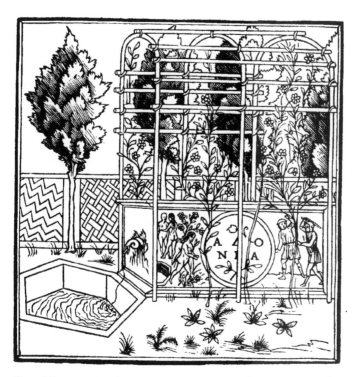

sopra il fonte. Nelquale aptamente era infixo uno ferpe aureo ficto ob-
repere fora duna latebrofa crepidine di faxo. Cum inuoluti uertigini, di
conueniente craffitudine euomeua largamente nel fonoro fonte la chia-
riffima aqua. Onde per tale magifterio il fignifico artifice, il ferpe haueua
fufo inglobato, per infrenare lo impeto dellaqua. Laquale per libero mea
to & directo fiftulato harebbe ultra gli limiti del fonte fparfo.

Sopra la plana del præfato fepulchro la Diuina Genitrice fedeua
puerpera exfcalpta, nó fencia fúmo ftupore di ptiofa petra Sardonyce tri
colore, fopra una fedula antiqria, nó excedéte la fua feffióe della fardoa ue
na, ma cú ícredibile iuéto & artificio era tutto il cythereo corpufculo della uéa lactea del onyce, qfi deueftito, p cħ folamte era relicto uno uelamine della rubra uena cælante lo arcano della natura, uelando parte di una
coxa, & il refiduo fopra la plana defcendeua. Demigrando pofcia fopra p

la papilla finiftra reluctantilo. Et dalle fpalle reuoltate allaqua depédulo accufaua imitante cum mirabile fcalptura ,niente di meno gli fancti mébri, effa amplexando lactabonda Cupidine,cum il fimulachro il mater no affecto indicante,cum gratiofa coloratione delle gene dambidui della rubente uena,cum la tatula dextra. O belliffima operatura da contempla re miraculofa. Solamente del fpirito uitale diminuta, Cum la difcrimina ta fronte dagli annulanti capilli fopra le piane tempore ,& dalloccipitio, cum uno nodulario ligamine compofitamente ingrumati. La parte foluta dindi fe extendeua fina al federe pápinulanti. Et di fcalptura exacti gli ftrumuli,cum gli uertigini peruii di trepanario conato egregiamente expreffi. Referuati della uena Sardoa tranflucida illucente. Quale del foe lice Polycrate nel delubro della concordia,nel aureo corno íclufa da Au gufto non fue dicata. Il finiftro peduculo teniua al feder ritracto,& laltro allextimo,ouero limbo della plana protenfo. Il quale fancto pede,
le nymphe cernue geniculate prolapfe,& nui,fue fumma cú
religione deofculato. Sotto del quale peciolo. Nella co
ronicula,era reftata una,fafcicula di liniamé
to expedita. Et in quefta di paruicu
le litere noftrate,annotato
uidi tale difti-
chon.
Non lac fæue puer,lachrymas fed fugis amaras,
Reddendas matri,cariq; Adonis amore.

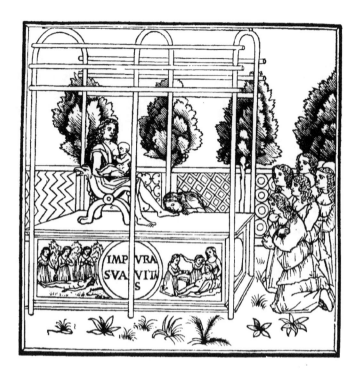

Facto & pacta debitamnte questa honoraria & diuota cerimonia, sora
uscissimo della sacrata pguletta. Le inclyte nymphe cum affabile facun‑
dia a noi dissero. Sapiate che il psente loco e mysterioso, & di maximo ue
nerato celeberrimo, Et in omni anno anniuersariamente il pridiano di
delle calende di Magio, Veni quiui la Diuina matre, cum il dilecto filio,
cum diuía pompa di lustratione, & cum essa tute nui sue subdite, & al suo
imperio ultronee cum obseruato famulitio, & cum superba solemnitate
conuenimo. Peruenuta dunque quiui cum suaue lachryme & suspiruli.
Da nui impera, che tutte le rose della pergula, & denudati, ancora gli can‑
celli di quelle fiano, & sopra il sepulchro alabastriceo, cum inuocatione
altisone ritualmente spargere, & congestitiamente coprire. Poscia
cum il dicto ordine, & processo primo se parte. Nel sequente di ca‑
lendario gli spoliati rosarii se reflorano al numero di rose candente.
Et ad gli idi un altra fiata la dea cum il modo primo retornando. E di‑

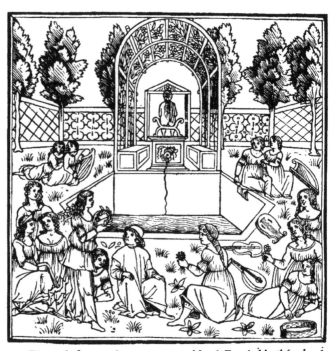

Finito che la nympha cum comitate blandissima hebbe il suo beni
gno suaso & multo acceptissima recordatiōe , che la mia acrocoma Polia
propera & māsuetissima leuato se cum gli sui festeuoli ,& facetissimi simu
lachri ,ouero sembianti,& cum punicante gene,& rubéte buccule da ho
nesto & uenerāte rubore suffuse aptauase di uolere per omni uia satissare
di natura prompta ad omni uirtute,& dare opera alla honesta petitionẻ.
Non che prima peroe se potesse cælare & dicio retinere alquāto che ella
intrinsicamente non suspirulasse.Ilquale dulcissimo suspirulo penetroe
reflectendo nel intimo del mio,immo suo core,per la uniforme conuenientia.   Quale aduene a dui parimente participati & concordi litui. Et
ciascuna cum diuo obtuto respecta intrepidulamente,cum quegli ludi-
bondi & micanti ochii,Da fare (Ome)gli adamanti fresi in mille fragmé
ticuli.Cum pie & summisse uoce,& cum elegantissimi gesti decentemen
te reuerita ogni una , ritornoe al suo solatioso sedere supra il serpilaceo so
lo.La initiata opera sequendo sellularia . Cum accommodata pronunti
atio-

NOTES

1.   For background see Frederic C. Lane, *Venice: A Maritime Republic* (Baltimore, MD and London: Johns Hopkins University Press, 1977), pp. 202-49; and Margaret King, *Venetian Humanism in an Age of Patrician Dominance* (Princeton, NJ: Princeton University Press, 1986).

2.   George Painter, *The Hypnerotomachia Poliphili of 1499: An Introduction to the Dream, the Dreamer, the Artist and the Printer*, 2 vols. (London: Eugrammia Press 1963), 1:3.

3.   In one of those coincidences of history, a little more than five hundred years from the date of the first printed book, in his *Understanding Media* (New York: McGraw-Hill, 1964), Marshall McLuhan predicted that the wave of the future would be away from the cool printed word and towards the hot media, like television, which would create the global village of our times. An insult of the sixties was the epithet, "linear-oriented print freak" regarding those who had become dependent upon print to the detriment of a more inclusive sensory approach to experience.

4.   Elizabeth Eisenstein, *Printing Revolution in Early Modern Europe* (Cambridge: Cambridge University Press, 1983), pp. 204, 206.

5.   Horatio Brown in his *The Venetian Printing Press: 1469-1800* (1891; reprint, Amsterdam: Gérard Th. van Heusden, 1969), p. 50, gives the following figures: Rome, 41; Florence, 37; Milan, 63; Naples, 27; Venice, 207.

6.   *Per la storia del libro in Italia nei secoli xv e xvi* (Florence: Leo S. Olski, 1900), p. 5.

7.   Jacob Burckhardt, *The Civilization of the Renaissance in Italy* (London: Phaidon, 1965), p. 117.

8.   S. H. Steinberg, *Five Hundred Years of Printing* (Harmondsworth: Penguin, 1955), p. 40. Traveling the old route via Augsburg, Sweinheim and Pannartz would have come to the abbey of Sts. Ulric and Afra, which maintained extremely close ties with the abbey at Subiaco, since both excelled in the high quality of works that emanated from their scriptoria.

9.   Hellmut Lehmann-Haupt, *Peter Schoeffer of Gernsheim and Mainz* (Rochester, NY: L. Hart, 1950), p. 75.

10.   These were Donatus, *Latin Grammar* (1464); Cicero, *De oratore* (1465); Lactantius, *Opera* (1465); and Augustine, *De civitate Dei* (1467).

11.   "Centesimus autem quadragesium septimus ab Aldi ave natali agitur annus" in the preface to *De morte dialogus* by A.

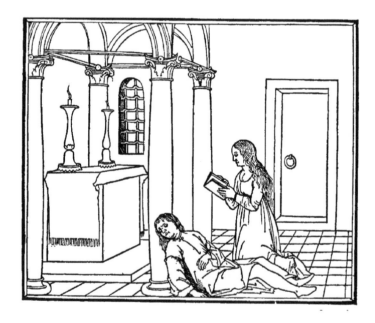

P. Parisinus. This reference to Aldus the Elder's birthdate was brought to light in 1804 by Abbot Antonmaria Amoretti in a privately printed pamphlet. Abbot Amoretti, however, holds that the Latin verb *agitur* means that the 147th year from Aldus' birth had not just begun, but had run its course, and therefore his birth year should be advanced to 1449. Some accept that argument; others like Horatio Brown, or Edward Robertson in his commemorative *Aldus Manutius, the Scholar Printer,*

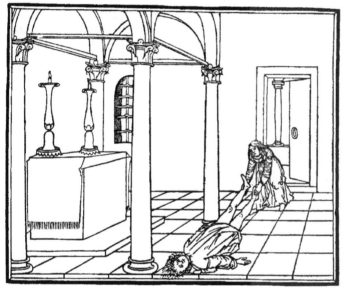

1450-1515 (Manchester: Manchester University Press, 1950), take 1450 as the more probable date.

12.   Leonardas Gerulaitis, "The Venetian Incunabula: Printers and Readers" (Ph.D. dissertation, University of Michigan, 1969), p. 127.

13.   Ibid, p. 126.

14.   See, for example, Paul Oskar Kristeller, *Renaissance Thought* (New York: Harper & Row, 1961); Eugenio Garin, *Italian Humanism* (New York: Harper & Row, 1965); or Denys Hay and John Law, *Italy in the Age of the Renaissance* (London and New York: Longman, 1989).

15.   Steinberg, p. 17.

16.   Margaret Aston, *The Fifteenth Century* (London: Thames & Hudson, 1968), p. 82.

17.   France has led the way in scholarship on Aldus. The most comprehensive works are: Antoine Augustin Renouard, *Annales de l'Imprimerie des Alde* (Paris: J. Renouard, 1834); Pierre de Nolhac, *Les correspondants de Alde Manuce* (1887-88; reprint, Turin: Bottega d'Erasmo, 1961); Armand Baschet, *Aldo Manuzio: Lettres et documents* (Venice: Antonelli, 1867); Ambroise Firmin-Didot, *Alde Manuce et l'Hellenisme à Venise* (1875; reprint, Brussels: Culture et Civilisation, 1966).

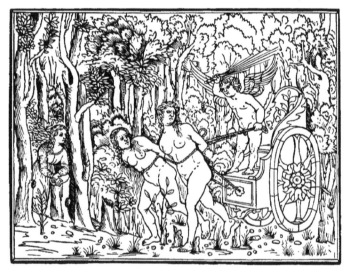

18.   John Aldington Symonds, *Renaissance in Italy*, 7 vols. (London: Smith, Elder, 1875-86), 2:362.

19.   Mario Ferrigni, *Aldo Manuzio* (Milan: Alpes, 1925), p. 21.

20.   G. P. Winship, *Printing in the Fifteenth Century* (Philadelphia, PA: University of Pennsylvania Press, 1940), p. 72. A certain Dr. Hartmann Schedel of Nuremberg, who visited Rome when the Sweinheim and Pannartz press was at Palazzo Massimo, examined their publications and made notes of titles and prices so that he could send for them from Germany. The prices are in papal ducats: Lucan, 1 ducat; Virgil, 2; St. Augustine, 5; Livy, 7; Pliny, 8; the Bible in Latin, 10. Schedel was later to be the famed publisher of Anton Koberger's *Nuremberg Chronicle*, whose woodcut views of Italian cities provide us with some of our best historical images of Rome, Florence, and Venice.

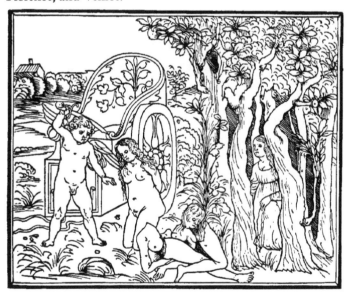

21.   Eugenio Garin, *Prosatori Latini dei '400* (Milan: R. Ricciardi, 1952), p. 599.

22.   John Philip Edmon, "Conrad Sweynheym and Arnold Pannartz, the First Roman Printers," *Papers of the Edinburgh Bibliographical Society* 9 (1904⁄13): 13.

23.   Steinberg, p. 51.

24.   See, for example, the interpretations of John F. D'Amico, *Renaissance Humanism in Papal Rome* (Baltimore, MD: Johns Hopkins University Press, 1983); Phyllis W. G. Gordon, *Two Renaissance Bookhunters* (New York: Columbia University Press, 1974 and 1991); and John W. O'Malley, *Praise and Blame in Renaissance Rome* (Durham, NC: Duke University Press, 1979).

25.   Symonds, pp. 215⁄18.

26.   Known as Pomponius Laetus, having latinized his sur⁄name and added the qualifying adjective, *laetus*, to describe his genial disposition. After his misfortune in earning the enmity of Pope Paul II, his new qualifier became *Infortunatus*.

27.   Tonino Gualdi, *Il quinto centenario della nascita di Aldo Pio Romano cittadino di Carpi* (Carpi: Civic Museum, n.d.), based on a talk given October 2, 1949 in Carpi.

28.   Ferrigni, p. 54.

29.   Gordon, pp. 10, 198.

30.   Prologue to the *Thesaurus cornucopiae* translated from Latin into English by Antje Lemke, in *Aldus Manutius and His* Thesaurus cornucopiae *of 1496* (Syracuse, NY: Syracuse University Press, 1958), p. 11.

31.   Brown, pp. 36⁄39.

32.   Martin J. C. Lowry, *The World of Aldus Manutius: Business and Scholarship in Renaissance Venice* (Ithaca, NY: Cornell University Press, 1979), p. 56.

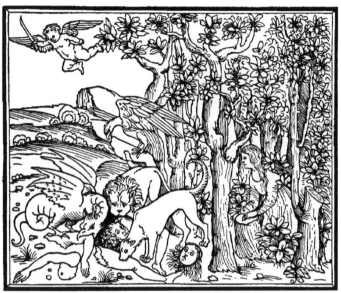

33.   Harry George Fletcher, *New Aldine Studies* (San Francisco: Bernard M. Rosenthal, 1988), p. 29.

34.   Hay and Law, pp. 163-68.

35.   Dazzi, p. 25.

36.   Edmund Goldsmid, *The Aldine Press* (Edinburgh:
privately printed, 1887), 1:31.

37.   Fletcher, p. 88.

38.   Fletcher, pp. 90-91.

39.   Fletcher, p. 43.

40.   Manlio Dazzi, *Aldo Manuzio e il dialogo Veneziano di
Erasmo* (Vicenza: Neri Pozza Editore, 1969), p. 156. See also
Margaret Mann Phillips, *The Adages of Erasmus* (Cambridge:
Cambridge University Press, 1964), pp. 171-90.

41.   According to the announcement of Edizioni Ristampe
Anastatiche, which oversaw a reprint edition some years ago,

only one extant copy of the *Hypnerotomachia Poliphili* is known to carry the dedicatory poem, and that is the copy of the Deutsche Staatsbibliothek of Berlin.

42. Charles Reade, *The Cloister and the Hearth* (New York: Dodd, Mead, 1928), pp. 448, 519-28.

43. Dazzi, p. 55 n. 83.

44. Edgar Wind, *Pagan Mysteries in the Renaissance* (Harmondsworth: Penguin, 1967), p. 24.

45. Franceso Colonna, *Hypnerotomachia Poliphili*, ed. Giovanni Pozzi and Lucia Ciapponi, 2 vols. (Padua: Editrice Antenore, 1964), 2:234. The commentary to the text where Colonna refers to "the noble Lelio family" shows that the reference is to the actual Lelli family of Treviso.

46. Edmund Wilson, *Axel's Castle* (New York: Scribner's, 1931), p. 229.

47. Philip Hofer, "Variant Copies of the 1499 Poliphilus," *Bulletin of the New York Public Library* 36 (June 1932): 475-86.

48. Painter, 1:10-11, identifies erasures and defacings to the Satyr (e7 recto, p. 13 above), Leda and the Swan (k7 verso, p. 60), Priapus (m6 recto, p. 77), and the Herm (x8 verso, p. 174).

49. Regarding the plate entitled "The Rustic Altar of Priapus" (p. 77), J. W. Appell, *The Dream of Poliphilus* (London: W. Griggs, 1893), p. 10, comments: "In the original copies this famous woodcut, which occupies the entire page, is usually torn or disfigured by ink."

50. See n. 45 above.

51. William Dana Orcutt, *The Book in Italy* (London: George G. Harrap, 1928), p. 91.

52. Linda Fierz-David, *The Dream of Poliphilo: The Soul in Love,* trans. Mary Hottinger (New York: Pantheon, 1950), p. 238.

53. Lowry, p. 122.
54. Wind, pp. 103-4.
55. Dazzi, pp. 39-40.
56. Ferrigni, pp. 168, 180.
57. Elizabeth Eisenstein, *The Printing Press as an Agent of*

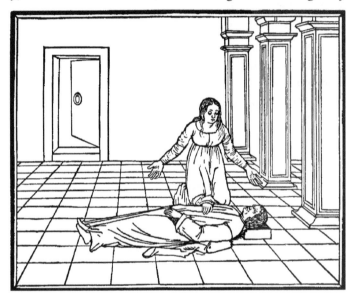

Change (Cambridge: Cambridge University Press, 1979), p. 219.
58. Dazzi, p. 119.
59. See Deno J. Geanakoplos, "Erasmus and the Aldine Academy of Venice," *Greek, Roman and Byzantine Studies* 3 (1960): 107-34.
60. Ferrigni, p. 222.
61. James Bruce Ross, *The Portable Renaissance Reader* (New York: Viking, 1953), p. 396.

62.   Redmont Burke, "The Most Beautiful Book of the Fifteenth Century," *Bulletin of the New York Public Library* 58
(Sept. 1954): 419-28.

63.   Lowry, p. 306.

64.   Curt F. Buhler, "Aldus Manutius," *Bibliographical
Society of America Papers* 44 (1950): 210.

65.   Matteo Bandello, *Tutte le opere,* ed. Francesco Flora, 2
vols. (Milan: Mondadori, 1952), p. 777. Novella XV is preceded
by a dedicatory letter to "the most learned Aldo Pio Manuzio
Romano."

66.   Ferrigni, p. 240.

*

* *

*

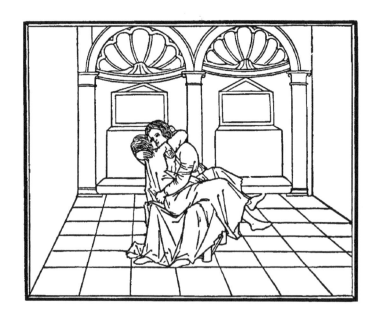

BIBLIOGRAPHY

Aldus Manutius

Ahmanson-Murphy, University of California at Los Angeles. *The Ahmanson-Murphy Aldine Collection: A Checklist of the Books from the Press of Aldo Pio Manuzio.* Compiled by Brooke Whiting. Los Angeles, CA: U.C.L.A. Research Library, 1985.

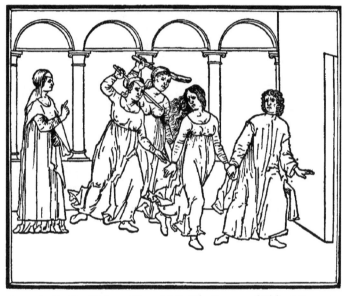

Angerhofer, Paul J. In aedibus Aldi: *The Legacy of Aldus Manutius and His Press.* Provo, UT: Friends of the Harold B. Lee Library, 1995.
Barker, Nicolas. *Aldus Manutius and the Development of Greek Script & Type in the Fifteenth Century.* Sandy Hook, CT: Chiswick Book Shop, 1985.
—. *Aldus Manutius. Mercantile Empire of the Intellect.* Los Angeles: University Research Library, UCLA, 1989.

Blumenthal, Joseph. *Art of the Printed Book, 1455-1955.* Boston: David Godine, 1973.

Brown, Horatio F. The V*enetian Printing Press.* London, 1891. Reprint. Amsterdam: Gérard Th. van Heusden, 1969.

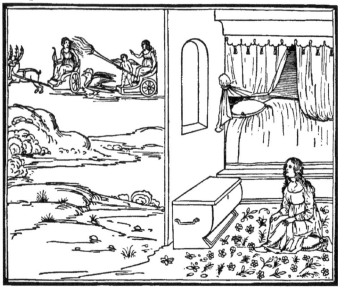

Buhler, Curt F. *Fifteenth Century Books and the Twentieth Century.* New York: Grolier Club, 1952.

—. *Early Books and Manuscripts.* New York: Grolier Club, 1973.

Davies, Martin. *Aldus Manutius. The Printer and Publisher of Renaissance Venice.* London: British Library, 1995.

DeVinne, Theodore Low. *Notable Printers of Italy During the Fifteenth Century.* New York: De Vinne Press, 1910.

—. *The First Editor: Aldus Pius Manutius.* New York: Targ, 1983.

Dionisotti, Carlo. *Aldo Manuzio. Umanista e Editore.* Milan: Edizioni il Polifilo, 1995.

Fletcher, Harry George. *In Praise of Aldus Manutius: A Quincentenary Exhibition.* New York: Pierpont Morgan Library, 1995.

—. *New Aldine Studies: Documentary Essays on the Life and Works of Aldus Manutius.* San Francisco: Bernard M. Rosenthal, 1988.

Geanakoplos, Deno John. *Greek Scholars in Venice.* Cambridge, MA: Harvard University Press, 1962.

Gerulaitis, Leonardas V. *Printing and Publishing in Fifteenth-Century Venice.* Chicago: American Library Association, 1976.

Goldsmid, Edmund. *The Aldine Press.* Edinburgh: privately printed, 1887.

Grendler, Paul F. *Aldus Manutius: Humanist, Teacher, and Printer.* Providence, RI: John Carter Brown Library, 1984.

Lemke, Antje. *Aldus Manutius and His* Thesaurus cornucopiae *of 1496.* Syracuse, NY: Syracuse University Press, 1958.

Lowry, Martin J.C. *The World of Aldus Manutius: Business and Scholarship in Renaissance Venice.* Ithaca, NY: Cornell University Press, 1979.

Norton, Frederick John. *Italian Printers, 1501-1520.* London: Bowes & Bowes, 1958.

Orcutt, William Dana. *The Book in Italy During the 15th and 16th Centuries.* New York: Harper & Brothers, 1928.

Proctor, Robert. *The Printing of Greek in the Fifteenth Century.* Oxford: Oxford University Press for the Bibliographic Society, 1900.

Robertson, Edward. *Aldus Manutius, the Scholar-Printer, 1450-1515.* Manchester: Manchester University Press, 1950.

Steinberg, S. H. *Five Hundred Years of Printing.* New Castle, DE: Oak Knoll, 1996.

Stubbs, John O. *et al.,* eds. Festina lente. *A Celebration of the Wosk-McDonald Aldine Collection at SFU.* Burnaby, BC: SFU Friends of the Library, 1996.

Winship, George P. *Printing in the 15th Century.* Philadelphia, PA: University of Pennsylvania Press, 1940.

—. *Gutenberg to Plantin.* Cambridge, MA: Harvard University Press, 1926.

Zeidberg, D.S. *et al.,* eds. *Aldus Manutius and Renaissance Culture.* Florence: L.S. Olschki, 1998.

HYPNEROTOMACHIA POLIPHILI

Editions

Colonna, Francesco. *Hypnerotomachia Poliphili ubi humana omnia nisi somnium esse docet.* Venice: Aldus, 1499.

—. *La Hypnerotomachia Di Poliphilo. Cioè Pugna D'Amore in Sogno. Dov' Egli Mostra, che Tutte Le Cose Humane Non Sono Altro Che Sogno.* Venice: Figliuoli di Aldo, 1545.

—. *Hypnerotomachie. Ou Discours du songe De Poliphile... Nouvellement traduict de langage Italien en François.* Paris: for Iaques Kerver, 1546. Reprint 1554. Reprint, Auxerre: Bibliothèque Municipale, 2000.

—. *Hypnerotomachie, ou Discours du Songe de Poliphile, deduisant comme Amour le combat à l'occasion de Polia...* Jacques Gohory and Jean Martin, eds. Cardinal de Lenoncourt, trans. Paris: I. Le Blanc for Iaques Kerver, 1561. Reprint, Bertram Guégan, ed. Paris: Payot, 1926.

—. *Hypnerotomachia. The Strife of Love in a Dream.* Robert Dallington, trans. London: John Charlewood for Simon Waterson and William Holme, 1592. Reprint, Lucy Gent, ed. Delmar, NY: Scholar's Fascimiles and Reprints, 1973. Reprint, New York: Garland, 1976.

—. *Le tableau des riches inventions couverts du voile des feintes amoureuses, qui sont representées dans le Songe de Poliphile desvoilées des ombres du Songe & subtilement exposées.* Béroalde de Verville, trans. Paris: Mattieu Guillemot, 1600.

—. *Songe de Poliphile.* J. G. Legrand, trans. Paris: P. Didot l'aîné, 1804. Reprint, Parma: Bodoni, 1811.

—. *Le Songe de Poliphile, ou Hypnerotomachie de frère F. Colonna, Littéralement traduit pour le première fois.* Claude Popelin, ed. and trans. 2 vols. Paris: I. Liseux, 1880-83. Reprint, Geneva: Slatkine, 1994.

—. Reprint of Venice 1499 ed. J. W. Appell, trans. London: Privy Council, Dept. of Science and Art in Photo-Lithography, 1888. Second ed. W. Griggs, ed., 1893.

—. *The Strife of Love in a Dream, being the Elizabethan Version of the First Book of the Hypnerotomachia Poliphili of Francesco Colonna.* Andrew Lang, ed. London: D. Nutt, 1890.

—. *Hypnerotomachia Poliphili.* London: Methuen, 1901 and 1904. Facs. reprint of 1499 edition.

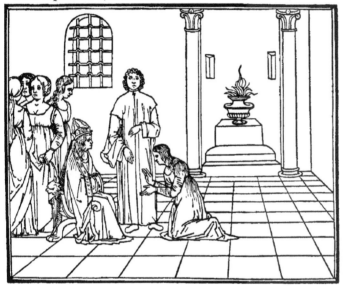

—. In *Opere di Jacopo Sannazaro, con saggi dell' Hyp. Pol. di Fr. Col. e del Peregrino di Jacopo Caviceo.* Enrico Carrara, ed. Turin: UTET, 1952. Reprint, 1967.

—. *The Hypnerotomachia Poliphili of 1499: An Introduction to the Dream, the Dreamer, the Artist and the Printer.* George Painter, ed. 2 vols. London: Eugrammia Press, 1963. Vol. 2.

—. *Hypnerotomachia Poliphili ubi humana omnia nisi somnium esse docet.* Farnborough, Hants.: Gregg International, 1969. (1499 ed.)

—. *Hypnerotomachia Poliphili ubi humana omnia nisi somnium esse docet.* Giovanni Pozzi and Lucia Ciapponi, eds. 2 vols. Padova: Antenore, 1964. Reprint, 1980. Vol. 1. (1499 ed.)

——. *Hypnerotomachia Poliphili.* Marco Ariani and Mino Gabriele, eds. Milan: Adelphi, 1998.

——. *Hypnerotomachia Poliphili. The Strife of Love in a Dream.* Trans. and ed. Joscelyn Godwin. New York: Thames & Hudson, 1999.

Selected Studies

Appell, J. W. *Introductory Notes and Description to the Dream of Poliphilus.* London: W. Griggs, 1893.

Fierz-David, Linda. *The Dream of Poliphilo.* Mary Hottinger, trans. New York: Pantheon, 1950.

Haebler, Konrad. *The Study of Incunabula.* New York: Kraus, 1967.

Painter, George. *The Hypnerotomachia Poliphili of 1499: An Introduction to the Dream, the Dreamer, the Artist and the Printer.* 2 vols. London: Eugrammia Press, 1963. Vol. 1.

Pérez-Gómez, Alberto. *Polyphilo, or, The Dark Forest Revisited. An Erotic Epiphany of Architecture.* Cambridge, MA: MIT Press, 1992.

Pollard, Alfred W. *Italian Book Illustrations.* Reprint. New York: Burt Franklin, 1973.

——. *Fine Books.* Reprint. New York: Cooper Square, 1964.

Pozzi, Giovanni. *Francesco Colonna und Aldo Manuzio.* Bern: The Monotype Corporation, 1962.

—— and Lucia Ciapponi, eds. *Hypnerotomachia Poliphili ubi humana omnia nisi somnium esse docet.* 2 vols. Padova: Antenore, 1964. Reprint, 1980. Vol. 2.

Wind, Edgar. *Pagan Mysteries in the Renaissance.* Rev. ed. Harmondsworth: Penguin, 1967.

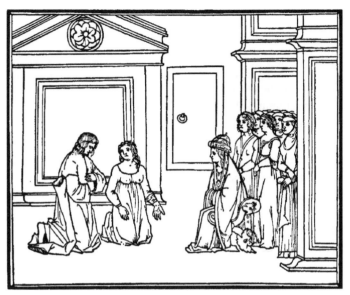

ILLUSTRATIONS

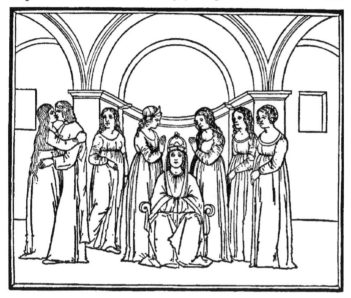

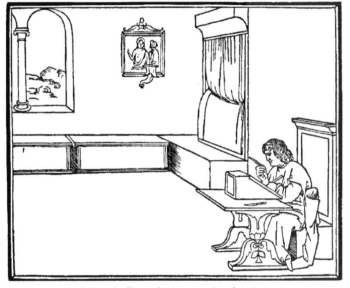

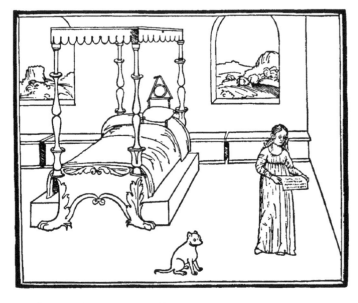

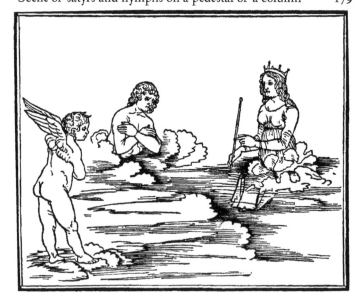

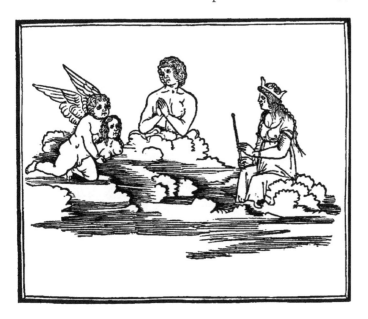

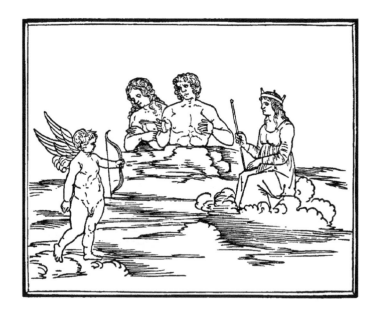

INDEX

The First Printing of This Book Was Completed on August 15, 1991 at Italica Press, New York City. It Was Composed on a Macintosh System Using Aldus PageMaker 4.0 and Set in Adobe Garamond. This Fourth Printing Was Completed on July 6, 2008 in New York City. It Was Composed on a Macintoch System Using Adobe InDesign CS2. and Set in Adobe Garamond and Poliphilus. It Was Printed on 60-lb., Acid-Free Paper by LightningSource, U. S. A./ E. U.
* *

*

Lightning Source UK Ltd.
Milton Keynes UK
UKHW010852030521
383015UK00001B/247